The
Adult Longeing
Guide

Exercises to Build an Independent Seat

Emily Esterson

THE LYONS PRESS
Guilford, Connecticut
An Imprint of The Globe Pequot Press

The Lyons Press is an imprint of The Globe Pequot Press.

Models: Michelle Murphy, Janice Tiche, Penny Avery, Tere Carr, Nicole Thuengen-Polligkeit, Mary Sorensen

Library of Congress Cataloging-in-Publication Data

Esterson, Emily.
  The adult longeing guide : exercises to build an independent seat / Emily Esterson.
    p. cm.
  Includes bibliographical references and index.
  ISBN 978-1-59921-196-1 (alk. paper)
  1. Lungeing (Horsemanship) I. Title.
  SF287.E78 2008
  798.2—dc22

                                                                    2007049954

Printed in the United States of America

10 9 8 7 6 5 4 3 2 1

Contents

Introduction

A FEW YEARS AGO DURING A CLINIC IN WHICH I WAS PARTICIPATING, I SAT next to a woman whom I'd never met before, but who happened to live in my neighborhood. We started talking, and by the end of the morning, we'd made a plan: We'd schedule weekly longeing sessions to improve our riding.

For longer than I can remember, I've wanted only to be a good horsewoman. Forget having an interesting and successful career. Love life, too, was a secondary consideration. My goal has been to ride beautifully and effectively, to care for horses well, and to live in an environment where we could all thrive. Call me a narcissist, but I wanted all the people standing on the rail at the horse show (any horse show) to make admiring *oohs* and *ahs* when I rode into the ring. I visualized riding like Olympic dressage champion Anky van Grunsven, even though I am quite short and somewhat plump. It's hard to ride like a six-foot blond when you're five-foot-three and brunette (now salt-and-pepper). As much as I wanted to ride like Anky or three-day Olympic eventer Denny Emerson (my hero and occasional clinician when I was a younger, braver event rider), I was simply not long legged, and not very athletic.

It wasn't just ego that caused me to want to ride better. The more I learned about riding, horses, and the art of horsemanship, the more I became aware of the torture a poor seat was for a horse. More than anything, I've wanted my horses to love me and respond to me. All I've ever really cared about was the unconditional love of my horses.

In retrospect, I think the idea for the *Adult Longeing Guide* germinated twenty years ago, long before I became a professional writer, and long before I got serious about dressage. I learned to ride in the typical American school of horsemanship: A first ride at age five on Cape Cod near the family summer home; then group lessons at a pony barn to which my New York City born-and-bred mother patiently drove me every single Saturday morning; and summer camp, where I had to be encouraged—no, forced, threatened, and cajoled—to participate in the other activities, like swimming, woodcraft, and pottery. I was not a well-rounded camper. All I wanted to do was stay at the stable.

I didn't even know you could longe a rider until I went to work for Janet and Henry Schurink in Vermont during college. The Dutch couple, and their son and daughter, Jerry and Renee, bred Trakehners. Janet showed FEI dressage and Henry managed the breeding operation. Jerry rode event horses and Renee taught local kids on a cadre of ill-tempered white ponies. It was my first exposure to European-style horsemanship, and I believe it was Janet who first suggested longeing to me. I was a hell-bent eventer and I didn't take a whole lot seriously at age twenty. Later I went to work as a groom for Janet "Dolly" Hannon and A. Whit Watkins, both ambitious dressage riders who were working toward riding and showing at the FEI levels. Dolly and Whit worked on the longe almost every Friday morning. They were incredibly dedicated to improving their riding by working on their seats.

I, however, still wasn't that dedicated to my position. I must have been terribly aware of my shortcomings because for years I refused to be videotaped riding. I knew what I would see: a plump rider with a big behind who drops her left shoulder, slumps habitually, and can't sit the trot. No Anky in *that* picture. I'd heard it a million times from a dozen instructors. I spent a lot of time avoiding working on my seat, just as people with addictions deny their problems. It made me feel bad to know I wasn't the graceful rider I wanted to be. So I just kept riding, never addressing the problem. After all, I'm a decent rider, my horses behave reasonably well, and I've been relatively competitive at eventing and dressage.

In my forties, something changed. If I had to pinpoint the moment I made the decision to finally listen to all those instructors who've passed through my life, ready to admit and work on my problems, it would have to be the day I bought Baleno at an auction. He's a really nice horse and, although I already had a nice, if aging, horse, Baleno would be competitive in the dressage ring. It became pretty obvious after the first year of owning Baleno that the only thing holding us back from moving up the levels was me—my seat, my leg, my hands. The first year I owned him, Baleno developed a big bald spot on his right flank from my busy leg. I learned quickly that if I was sitting tall and correctly, Baleno would do whatever I asked. If I was unbalanced, too heavy, or somehow out of timing, Baleno would not only *not* do what I asked, he would protest. He'd try to rub me off on the fence. I spent a year with a huge scrape on my knee, and went through two pairs of breeches.

And then I met Tere, at that clinic. We began longeing each other on my retired event horse, Volare. He's the perfect schoolmaster, since he's absolutely bombproof, is voice trained, and has a large canter that's easy to sit and a big open trot that isn't. My riding improved quite a bit once our longe lessons began. I wondered at the time why I waited until I was forty to actually get down to working on my seat.

Tere and I worked diligently every Sunday on our positions, and we made it up as we went along. I borrowed ideas from her—she's taught kids to ride on the longe line for years—as she did from me. Gradually we developed a vocabulary; some of the exercises got nicknames so we could use verbal shorthand to fix our shortcomings. My gripping knees, for example, were fixed with our "leg fluff" exercise (I later watched a Grand Prix freestyle on DVD and saw a rider canter down the center line, halt at X, and open both legs and slide them back behind her—the leg fluff in action). My leg is longer now and I no longer rub the hair off my horse's flank. Most days. I still struggle mightily with my seat, but now I catch the moments when I fall forward or forget my seat and leg and start pulling with the reins. I'm still no Anky, but I'm surely better than I was.

The most amazing part of my revelation was how much fun it was. The thirty minutes, at most, felt like exercising, riding, and hanging out with a friend all at once. It was a nice break from the intensity of schooling dressage and seemed a great opportunity just to focus on me for a while. Occasionally, Tere and I would get into a conversation about something unrelated to horses, while one of us was riding and the other longeing. We'd just keep talking, and somehow our riding, freed for the moment from intense scrutiny, would improve. Gradually we added exercises to the routine: Some days we'd work on sitting trot only for a few minutes, focusing instead on rising trot. Some days we worked on transitions. With my own students I mix it up a bit, adding canter, work in two point position, and longeing over small jumps. I'll ask them to leg yield in to a smaller circle and out to a larger one, so they can see that they don't need to use their reins to move the horse laterally, stop him, pick up a canter, do transitions, and work on the exercises in this book.

None of this is a revelation, especially for riders trained in Europe where longeing the rider is *de rigueur*. But it's my hope with this book that riding instructors, as well as adult riders who feel stuck, will get back to basics. After all, at the Spanish Riding School, students spend a year working on the longe. They trot, canter, ride without stirrups, and perform *haute école* movements, all without reins. Think how much happier all of our horses would be if we learned to ride with light rein contact and a better seat and leg.

Because I grew up like many other kids riding at summer camp on school horses, and later became a somewhat competent, but, more important, fearless twenty-something, green horses with all kinds of problems came my way. My position really suffered and continues to suffer. I'm still jealous of the Europeans with their very structured way of teaching riders to sit a horse. While researching this book, I watched Alexander Kottas's tape, *The Art of Classical Dressage with Arthur Kottas, Part 2, Lungeing the Rider* (they even did half pass, piaffe, passage, and flying changes on the longe line). The first sequence is his daughter, who must be eleven or twelve, being longed on a spectacular Haflinger. She has a wonderful, soft, competent seat, and I felt a jealousy unmatched since the days I rode school horses while other kids rode their *own* ponies. I also read the United States Pony Club manual, and several other technical books on longeing. I have long been a student of yoga, so many of the exercises here have been adapted from my yoga practice, and from the language of my teacher, Meta Hirshl, of YogaNow in Albuquerque. As I was writing this book, I coincidentally started taking African dance classes—mostly to break up my fitness routine. But I found ideas for exercises there, too. The traditions of West African dance involve a great deal of moving the hips one way, while moving the torso another way. It's about rhythm. Sound familiar?

As we've heard over and over, becoming a competent rider is a journey, not a destination. I'm still on that road, struggling with a left shoulder that drops and a right leg that crawls up. I spend a great deal of time working on these faults without stirrups and with a longeing partner whenever we can organize a session.

In Europe, longeing is seen as the only way to improve your seat. Riders don't just longe at the beginning of riding, but all through their riding careers, to work on and fix position problems. My hope is that *The Adult Longeing Guide* will encourage riders here to do the same.

Chapter 1
BEFORE YOU BEGIN

This copperplate engraving from Andreas Nunzer Gropaden (1603–1647) shows how longeing the rider has always been a part of the equestrian arts. (Credit: Wikimedia, public domain)

OVER THE PAST COUPLE OF DECADES, I'VE HEARD JUST ABOUT EVERY myth, half-truth, and truth about longeing. I've read a lot of good books about longeing, but few talk at any length about longeing the rider. Overall, I believe this subject is a little misunderstood in the United States. We think of it as a way to habituate children to horseback riding. It's common in beginning lesson programs, both for the young and the not-so-young. But after a rider can sit the trot and canter competently on the longe line, we set them free. Often adult riders plateau—they remain permanently at, say, first level in dressage, or in the same height class in the hunter ring. Some adults get stuck emotionally, battling back the same old fears every time they ride.

Longeing the adult rider is the perfect way to work over and beyond the inevitable stuck places in riding. While you certainly can, and should, longe young riders, my focus here is on helping adults. We all develop habits, especially those of us who ride by ourselves day in and day out. Longeing breaks up the riding routine, and helps adults conquer those automatic physical responses we develop when we don't have an instructor yelling at us all the time. It's also an opportunity to invite a friend over for a low-key horse date.

LONGEING IDEOLOGY DEBUNKED

1) It's spelled *lungeing* or *lunging.*

The *American Heritage Dictionary* doesn't have an equestrian definition of longeing. That's because it's the phonetic spelling of the French word *longe*, which derives from the Latin *longa* (long rein) and the French verb *allonger,* to elongate or lengthen, as in an elongated rein. Therefore, the proper spelling should be *longe*. We've adopted, here in the United States and in other English-speaking countries, the word *lunge* to describe the activity, but that's not technically correct. To demonstrate how deeply we disagree on the spelling, note that I have four books on my desk: two use *longeing* and two use *lungeing.* Go figure. One is a translation of a German book, another is the United States Pony Club manual. So even such authorities can't seem to agree. The word *lungeing* has always bothered me. It conjures up an image of exercise class at the gym. Partly because of that mental picture and partly because I've studied and lived in France, I chose *longe* and *longeing* for this book.

Longeur, however, is a different story. This is an Anglicization of *longe*, but as much as we like to add *eur* onto the end of French words it's not a correct grammatical construction. In fact, the correct word would be *longueur*, in which the "g" is hard, as in *long-err*, which actually translates to "length." Nonetheless, the United States Equestrian Federation adopted the word to describe the person holding the line in the discipline of vaulting, and hence we've adopted it here, as well.

2) Longeing is only for beginners.

Hopefuls have to pass a riding audition to be accepted into the Spanish Riding School in Vienna. Even though most, if not all, already have training, these young equestrians spend their entire first year riding on the longe. They learn (or relearn) to walk, trot, canter, half-halt, half pass, flying change, and even perform the *haute école* movements attached to a line. Longeing teaches them to have a fully independent seat and leg, soft quiet hands that guide rather than pull, and an impeccable seat.

Top riders all over the world spend time on the longe trying to improve. Having someone longe a rider on a knowledgeable horse can help her develop better harmony and more sensitivity to the horse. It seems, however, that in the United States we're loath to return to the longe because there's a perception that this activity is only for beginners. A trainer from Germany, a *bereiter* ("teacher of teachers"), Nicole Thuengen-Polligkeit, came to our humble boarding stable in New Mexico three times a year. Nicole regularly saw riders who wanted to improve their seats but didn't have the tools. Instead of continuing to struggle, clinic after clinic, with the same faults, she decided to give us a longeing primer so we could work together after she'd returned to Germany. After an initial session on proper technique, we paired off, two riders and a horse, and she critiqued the longeur's technique, noting precisely where the longeur should be on the circle and what she should be doing with her whip. Nicole then recommended exercises that would suit each rider's particular problem. All the participants were adult riders who had a fair amount of experience.

The purpose of the longe lesson is manifold: to work on the rider's seat; to educate the rider on the aids; to develop strength and fitness; to loosen up and relax the tense rider; to calm the nervous rider; to meditate; to self-focus for twenty minutes. And also to have fun.

3) Longeing is for dressage riders.

You're out on a trail ride, just poking along and chatting with your friend. A deer bolts out of the woods, startling your horse. You don't really have time to grab the horn or mane or martingale strap, but since you've been taking longe lessons, you remember to grow tall and deep in the saddle and you weather the spook without becoming unseated.

You're on mile fifty of a hundred-mile endurance ride. Everyone's feeling the pain, and your normally surefooted Arabian stumbles hard. Because you've been working on your stability in the saddle, you stay upright, helping the horse to balance. This potentially dangerous situation is minimized. You continue on your way.

Years ago, you fell off a horse while picking up the canter. Although you may not have been badly injured *physically*, your confidence hasn't been the same since. You tend to become nervous, and instead of a enjoying a nice floating canter (or any other gait, for that matter), you find yourself pinching with your thighs, holding your breath, and are scared out of your wits. Longeing could remedy this problem, building a comfortable rapport with riding again simply by learning that it's quite possible to control your body and your horse more effectively. So whether you're a fearful rider, a tense rider, or just want to be better at whatever discipline you chose to pursue with your horses, longeing can help.

4) The purpose of longeing is to get the bucks out of my horse before I ride him.

I was sitting at dinner one night with an experienced horsewoman of the hunter/jumper persuasion. Another dinner guest, unfamiliar with horses and equestrian sports, asked what my book was about. I explained briefly. The horsewoman, however, piped up, saying that you longe a horse to get the "yah-yahs" out of him. While you should certainly make sure your horse isn't going to buck you off, using the longe for only this purpose really isn't correct. Longeing is a training tool, both for horse and rider. If the horse becomes habituated to bucking and galloping around every time you suit him up for a longeing session, you've basically trained him to do just that. If you've developed this habit in your horse, and you get in a situation where longeing just isn't possible, you may be in a fair bit of trouble.

Beyond that, though, longeing has a multitude of purposes—to train the horse, to train the rider, to introduce the young horse to tack, and to teach the experienced rider "feel," as states the official instruction handbook of the German National Equestrian Federation. Riders work for years to capture the sensation where riding is so subtle, and horse and rider so harmonious, that the rider merely breathes her commands. Longeing can help riders get beyond the "left leg back, right heel down" form of riding to a more organic partnership with their horses. We longe to improve the rider's seat, confidence, and aids.

5) Longeing is boring.

Sure, anything done without creativity is boring. If you trot around in a circle for twenty minutes and the longeur picks on your position, both you and the horse will be bored. Just as you vary your workout routine in the gym, so is it important to add interest and challenge to your longe line sessions. The idea is to longe often—an hour a year won't do it—but weekly sessions have to be compelling. That's where the exercises in this book can come in: they can give you ideas to "play" on the longe, add variety, and stretch your physical and psychological limits.

6) You can't learn to jump on the longe line.

Years ago, I rode at a jumping and eventing stable just outside of Paris. I spent about ten months taking biweekly lessons with an accomplished event rider. We spent a great deal of time practicing our jumping, often on the longe with no reins or stirrups. The stable had a small indoor school, and Monsieur Lucas would set up a series of smallish jumps with low standards around the outside track. He had an encyclopedic knowledge of jumping exercises, and while on the longe line, I jumped with my arms out to the side, my eyes closed, with no stirrups, and a zillion combinations thereof. This training helped me when I got into any kind of trouble while jumping—it also helped me to stay off my horse's mouth even if I got unseated. In fact, spending a few minutes on the longe every week can help a rider of any discipline, riding in any saddle, to learn to be more balanced, graceful, and kind. It strengthens your legs, hones your seat, builds a confident eye, and develops your timing—all skills that every rider, whether hunter or roper, could use.

Properly adjusted side reins allow the horse to stretch forward and over his topline.

7) It's bad for my horse's legs.

Well, yes and no. Longeing your horse for hours on end and with no leg protection or without changing directions can damage the tendons and joints, or at the very least put unnecessary wear on the horse's fragile leg structures. In moderation, and with the proper boots or wraps, longeing isn't dangerous or injurious. You can use leg protection to support the horse's legs: sports boots or wraps (correctly applied, of course), and if he has a tendency to overreach (step on his own heels) consider adding bell boots as well. Change directions frequently—every five or ten minutes. Warm the horse up off the longe line with a free, strong, forward walk, and older or stiff horses should also be asked to trot to loosen up. Never longe a horse that's too young, lame, sore, or unsound.

8) Western riders don't need to be longed. They can hold onto the horn.

Face it. It's automatic. Reach for the horn when something goes wrong. It's always nice to have something to hold onto, but wouldn't it be a lot better if you didn't need the horn? I've never heard of the horn of a Western saddle breaking off, but then again, what if it did? And if the horn did break off, some Western riders would be at a loss as to how to balance in a dicey situation. Beyond safety, though, the benefits of longeing for the Western rider are the same as for anyone else: confidence, better control of the aids, less dependence on the bit and reins, and more grace in the saddle.

9) I need special equipment.

Here's your official longeing checklist. You may have some of this in your tack room (and who doesn't have all kinds of stuff in their tack room?), but some of it you may need to buy.

- Longe line that's at least thirty feet long. Some lines are measured in meters, so you'll want one that's about ten meters or longer. At

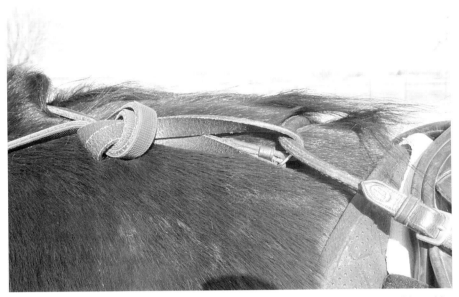

A bucking strap serves to keep the reins out of the way and to give the rider something with which to balance.

full extension, a thirty-foot longe line will give you a circle that's approximately twenty meters in diameter, which is large enough to be physically comfortable for horse and rider. Choose a longe line that's made of reinforced cotton or nylon webbing. I prefer the kind with a rubber donut at the end instead of a loop. It's tempting to put a hand through the loop, which isn't safe, but having a donut at the end stops the line from slipping through your hand while not entrapping it.

- Longe whip. You'll need to carry a long longe whip—at least fifteen feet from the handle to the end of the lash—long enough to encourage the horse but not so long or heavy that you'll fatigue your wrist. While most longe whips measure around fifteen to eighteen feet, some telescoping types measure longer. You should carry enough whip that your longeing horse understands what's being asked of him. Since you won't be using it to make contact with the horse, you don't need an excessively long one.

- Gloves

- Boots

- Helmet

- A longeing cavesson over a properly adjusted bridle (optional). You can get by with a properly adjusted halter, but it's not recommended, since you'll have a lot less control than if you use a cavesson.

- You can also longe from the bridle if you know how to do it correctly (see the next chapter on correct longeing techniques).

- Snaffle bit (never, ever longe a horse wearing any kind of Pelham, shank, or severe bit).

- Protective leg boots or wraps for the horse (optional). Many people don't wrap their horses' legs for longeing, but I recommend it.

- Properly adjusted side reins (optional). I like to use those with elastic ends, or with rubber donuts so they have some give to them. The side reins are used to give the horse the feeling of a steady, elastic rein contact as he's being longed. Using side reins allows the horse to use his back properly, which will make the horse more comfortable to ride. The side reins should be adjusted long enough to encourage the horse to stretch downward and forward, allowing him the full use of his neck and back muscles. Each time you change directions make sure the side reins are even. If the horse is well trained and doesn't tend to come above the bit (throw his head in the air), attach the side reins to the saddle's D-rings. If you want to work the horse and rider in a longer, stretchy frame, attach the side reins to the girth on both sides and then to the bit. For Western saddles, attach them to the rigging ring or the cinch. An additional note: remove the side reins for jumping exercises. Even though the exercises in this book only require the horse to jump a foot or two, side reins can inhibit the stretch in the horse's neck that allows him to jump in a balanced fashion.

- Bucking strap. A short piece of leather with clips on either end that attach to the D-rings of the saddle. It gives the rider a "handle" should she need to balance.

- Optional: A stirrup leather to put around the horse's neck for the rider to hold if needed, and a strap with a clip on both ends to keep the stirrups out of the way when they're crossed.

10) My horse isn't good enough to longe.
Keep in mind that you never, ever, longe a rider on a horse you don't know. Always test the horse on the longe without a rider first and then with an experienced rider aboard (and let the rider keep her reins, just in case), before you decide he's going to be your equine longeing partner.

THE HORSE

Speaking of horses, your ideal longeing partner doesn't spook—ever. If he does, it's the kind of laughable spook where he shakes his head a little bit. Your next-door neighbor could be getting ready to launch the next space shuttle, and this horse would barely blink at the commotion. Your perfect longeing horse partner also maintains a steady rhythm at all gaits. He doesn't rush into the canter or tumble on his nose when asked to walk. He's been taught to longe correctly, in that he knows it's work time, not galloping around and bucking time. This horse completely understands that when a rider is aboard, it's time to get down to business. He is well trained and light to the aids. He walks, trots, and canters at the request of the rider with a minimum of monkeying around. Certainly horses have good days and bad days, and they will act up. After all, they're beings with some modicum of free will. But overall, your perfect longeing horse will behave.

It bears repeating that your longeing partner should be the safest horse you can find. A voice-trained horse who knows what a half-halt is, has been trained to leg yield, and knows a little bit about jumping is ideal. Believe me, these horses do exist. If you have a horse that already longes quietly but hasn't yet been longed with a rider aboard, you may want to give him a test to see if he'll be suitable for this type of work. Have an experienced rider mount the horse. The longeur should also be very experienced; in case the horse becomes silly she'll know how to bring him under control. Test the horse by having the rider move around on the horse as a beginner might. Wiggle side to side, and gently and slowly move the arms up and down. Turn sideways and try to touch the horse's tail and mane. Try all kinds of movement at all three gaits to make sure there isn't a "spook button" at the trot that wasn't there at the walk. Take your time and test the horse thoroughly. If he doesn't do anything unexpected, he's probably a good longeing candidate.

A nervous horse may break into a bouncy, mini-trot, near-walk called a jig. If he jigs at the walk, he may be reacting to tension in the rider's seat or general demeanor. He could simply be excited or testing the situation. Or he could truly be unsuitable for longeing exercises because he's nervous. Both the rider and the longeur will have to work on deep, slow breathing and calmness, reassuring pats on the neck, and a gentle tug on the longe line. If

Properly attired and ready to longe, long-time friends Penny and Tere prepare for a session.

none of those techniques slows him to a steady walk rhythm, have the rider dismount and turn the horse out.

A horse that jigs can be rehabilitated for the longe if he generally behaves otherwise. Be sure to work with him with an experienced rider and longeur over a period of time to make sure the jigging isn't a habit or a reaction to pain.

SAFETY

Safety first, always. We've already talked about the perfect horse, which is the safest horse. But even bombproof horses startle. The longeur and the rider should take all possible precautions to assure the longeing experience is positive for everyone involved. Choose a good weather day. Although dedication is admirable, you rarely learn anything when the wind is blowing fifty miles per hour and it's twenty degrees outside. Assess how the rider is feeling. A sore back may be alleviated, for example, with some gentle walk exercises or may be exacerbated by riding in general. Make the experience enjoyable for all human and equine participants.

The rider, with helmet on and harness and chin strap fastened, wears boots and breeches, or boots, chaps (which, by the way, can inhibit the rider's movement), and jeans. The longeur can wear short or tall boots, if they're comfortable, and long pants or breeches, so she's ready when it's time to switch to the saddle. Long pants or breeches protect the ground person's legs should she trip or get accidentally dragged. Both rider and longeur should remove spurs. The longeur can trip on hers, and the rider will be doing so much moving around with her legs that having spurs would be quite dangerous should she accidentally bang the horse with them.

If for any reason the rider feels unseated, unbalanced, or otherwise like she might fall off, stop immediately and regroup. Horses can panic when riders do, so it's best to avoid this situation altogether with an immediate "whoa" command and a tug on the longe line. Never push a frightened rider past her limit unless she's clearly expressed that she wants you to. Otherwise, frightening the rider will make matters much worse.

Know Your Limits

The poses and exercises here can be modified for any body's limitations. As the longeur, you should evaluate the flexibility and physical confidence of any rider you work with and modify the exercises appropriately. As the rider, you should know how far is too far and not be afraid to express when you've had enough. Indeed, some of these exercises will ask riders to move their bodies in ways to which they may be unaccustomed. Riders who spend more time behind a desk than on a horse (which describes 90 percent of us, doesn't it?) will be physically more limited than those who ride half a dozen horses a day. And because this book is geared for desk jockeys rather than professional equestrians, I strongly encourage you to take the slow and steady approach. Better to work through to a good stretch; but not so far that the rider pulls a muscle or injures herself.

The same is true with confidence-building exercises. If your longeing partner is frightened or lacking confidence, take it slow. Overfacing a rider is a sure path to more intense fear, not more confidence. As we all know, horses sense what we're thinking when we're around them, so the best course of action for the fearful rider is a slow, incremental path to facing her emotional challenges. For example, if she's afraid of riding without her stirrups, she only needs to take a few steps without them to feel she's accomplished something. Adding additional steps of no-stirrup work as she feels comfortable will build her confidence, rather than shake it.

Let the rider stop now and then to evaluate what's happening with her body. The reason we work on longeing in the first place is to build body awareness, to feel how the tendons, muscles, and bones work with the horse's anatomy and how we can modify our own bodies to work in concert with our equine partners. We're working toward an independent, confident seat, not the Olympics.

This book is a guide, not a manual. The difference is that I'm making suggestions. It won't give you exhaustive numbers of exercises, because longeing sessions organically evolve. I've offered you numerous sequences, ideas for exercises, and ways to modify them, but I encourage you to experiment. The rider may want to work on stretches that aren't outlined here. She may have positional problems for which some movements are better than others. These are ideas to get you started, so I encourage you to work at your own pace, explore the exercises, and create your own if you're motivated to do so.

THE HUMAN

I've already talked about the perfect equine partner, but what about the perfect human cohort? Your longeing team should be compatible, first and foremost. Choose a fellow rider whose skills and eye you trust. You have to feel confident, if you're the one in the saddle, that the direction you're getting is valuable. Otherwise, you'll end up feeling as if your longe sessions aren't productive. It doesn't matter whether the person's skill level matches your own exactly—what you're after here is compatibility and a sense of curiosity and fun. Otherwise it's literally just going in circles. Pairs that don't generally work out are rider and longeur teams in which one person is frightened and the other confident. That automatically puts the confident person in the role of teacher/leader. We're looking for equality of mind, if not equality of skills.

Your partner should be able to gently correct you, without hurting your feelings. None of us is perfect; many of us have poor equitation habits. The longeur who can identify and gently suggest an improvement is much more valuable than one who criticizes unconstructively. A total, physical relationship with the horse through the seat, the legs, the breath, and the body overall is what we're after, and the longeur's main role is to guide the rider through the movements gently, but to also push the rider out of her comfort zone as often as possible. Praise frequently, and critique (rather than criticize) with suggestions for improvement. That's the motto.

Equipment and Technique

Earlier in this chapter I gave you a brief equipment list. Here's greater detail about how to use it correctly.

Saddle

You'll need a saddle that fits both riders, and that's equipped with a bucking strap or safety strap. Alternately, you can buckle an old stirrup leather snugly, but not tightly, around the horse's neck. Western riders can use the horn to stabilize. The rider can use the strap, horn, or leather to right herself should she lose her balance or to make herself more secure.

Riders with short arms who must slump forward to reach the bucking strap or mane may need to reach one hand behind themselves and place it on the cantle to stabilize. On the longe line, the hand that reaches for the cantle should always be the inside hand, unless instructed otherwise, to follow the horse's bend; the outside hand on the cantle will rotate the body to the outside and make it difficult for the longeur to keep the horse moving on the circle.

You'll need stirrup leathers that adjust enough to suit both riders; it's better not to have to roll the leathers to the right length for a shorter rider if you can avoid it. A hole punch is handy in case you need to make adjustments.

Bridle and Cavesson

Use only a snaffle bit on the bridle, not anything harsher. If you need a bridle with a stronger bit, you're probably using the wrong horse.

Most longeing books recommend using a cavesson over the bridle. It's a handy tool because it allows you to longe without interfering with the horse's mouth. Also, the longe line can be attached to the ring on the noseband of the cavesson, which allows the rider to perform some of the lateral movements described later on with more angle. Not all equestrianss have access to one. They also are notoriously difficult to adjust properly because some models have two throatlatches that must cross under the jaw. If not properly fitted, the noseband can slip down, inhibiting the nostrils. If you're not familiar with the proper fit and adjustment of a cavesson, I'd prefer you use a snaffle bridle with the longe line attached to the bit in one of the follow manners:

- If your horse is well trained, you can attach the longe line directly to the inside bit ring. Note, however, that when a horse pulls to the outside, the resistance of the longeur's hand on the line creates the action of the bit sliding *through* the horse's mouth. This method should only be used if the horse is very well trained and won't bolt (which should be the case with a good longeing horse anyway) or pull to the outside.

- One method is to attach the longe line to both the bit and the noseband, which gives you control while minimizing the action of pulling the bit through the horse's mouth. If you want to use this method you'll need a special longe line that has a loop rather than a snap at the end that can be slipped through the noseband and the snaffle ring.

The longe line can be run through the inside bit ring and attached to the outside ring. Alternately, the line can be looped through the inside once and then attached to the outside ring.

- You can run the line through the inside ring and pass it under the horse's chin, attaching it to the outside ring. This has an action similar to a curb chain, which can tighten against the horse's chin.

- A variation, both safe and recommended, is to loop the line once around the inside bit ring and snap it to the outside ring.

- You can also use a longeing strap, a short piece of leather or webbing that attaches to both sides of the bit ring. It has a small ring at the center to which you attach the longe line.

- You can also longe the horse with a halter, but this method offers the longeur the least amount of control.

- The final, least recommended method is to run the line through the inside bit ring and over the poll, attaching it to the outside ring. This is quite severe because any tug on the line is going to put pressure on the horse's poll *and* both bit rings. This is not recommended for our purposes—if you need this much control, you need a different horse.

The line in this case is run over the horse's poll and attached to the outside bit ring. This is the most severe method because it places pressure on both the bit and the horse's head.

Use the method you and the horse are most comfortable with.

Reins

During a longeing session, the reins need to be out of the way. Whether the rider has access to them depends on what you're doing. They can be tied out of the way in several fashions.

- They can be twisted and secured by slipping the throatlatch through them and reattaching the throatlatch buckle. In this way, the rider won't have any use of the reins at all, but you also won't risk them slipping forward.

- The second method is to leave the reins loose and knot them at the rider's end so she can take control if she needs it, but the reins are still out of the way.

- A third method is to unbuckle the reins, run them inside the bucking strap, and rebuckle them. In this case the reins should be long enough that they don't interfere with the horse's mouth at all unless and until the rider needs them.

To secure the reins but keep them accessible, unbuckle them, slip them through the bucking strap, and buckle them again.

- The fourth method is to knot the reins and run the unbuckled ends through the bucking strap. Then re-buckle them. This way, the reins are out of the way but still accessible.

Feel free to experiment with rein and longe line configurations to see which methods work best. You can also change the reins for different exercises; untwist and untie them for cantering or for lateral work, but keep them tied up for trot and walk. Some exercises will demand reins at the beginning, but the rider won't need them as frequently as she becomes more coordinated.

THE SESSION ITSELF

Choose an arena or area with soft footing. A round pen is fine as long as it's large enough that it doesn't put too much strain on the horse's legs. Gather your equipment, longe line coiled, whip in neutral position tucked behind you under your arm. The side reins are either clipped to each other over the horse's withers or not attached at all. The first rider mounts, adjusts her stirrups to the appropriate length, and asks the horse to walk and trot around the arena a few times on a long rein.

Once the horse is sufficiently loosened up, the horse and rider return to the center of the circle, where the longeur attaches the longe line to the bridle or cavesson, ties up the reins appropriately, and clips the side reins onto the bit rings. Then she adjusts their length. The side reins shouldn't be so tight that the horse has an enforced, short arch in his neck, but not so long that he'll have no contact with the bit no matter how far he stretches. He should be able to stretch forward and downward, arching gently over his back and into the bit. Keep the horse on a fairly large circle, retaining the extra line in your hand in a looping fashion so you can easily gather the line back in or pay it out. Never coil the line around your hand or arm.

Once you've attached the horse to the longe line, start out with a few circles of forward walk while the rider stretches out. A longeing session should never last more than twenty to thirty minutes, with the same parameters as any human exercise routine. It should include a few minutes of warm-up, a work session with rest breaks, and a few minutes of cooldown for maximum effectiveness. The most intense work happens in the middle of each rider's session. At the end of that rider's allotted ten or fifteen minutes (don't forget to wear a watch), let the horse and rider walk a couple of circles to relax the muscles as a cool down. Then you can switch riders and repeat, eliminating the first part of the session, walking and trotting off the longe. At this point, the horse should be warmed up enough to skip that step.

Change directions often and give both the rider and the horse frequent breaks. Keep it short, combining just a few of these exercises at a time, especially if both people want a chance to ride. Variety makes it fun and interesting and the experimentation stretches the rider's skill. Don't be afraid to vary different elements of the exercises to see what works and what best fits the pair. Some days you may just work on sitting trot without stirrups. Other days you may work on sitting trot, posting trot, and canter all in the same session. Vary the routine and go with what feels most useful at the time.

Chapter 2
WORK AT THE STANDSTILL

Imagine the typical twelve-year-old girl on horseback: "When can I canter? When can I learn to jump? Can I gallop now?" And bolder adults have wanted to feel that speed right away. Forget patient training. Let's just go! At summer camp many moons ago, our girls couldn't wait to get to the galloping road, a long, soft stretch of dirt through the woods where we counselors (against any good judgment) let the kids go for it. It was likely that we'd have one or two come off, but on a good day everyone stayed mounted and laughed and smiled about that gallop all the way home.

Indeed, our visions of horseback riding are always linked to the seductive, flying feeling of the gallop. But to get there confidently begins firmly at the standstill. That's right: the halt is where I start this book, because here the rider is usually free of worry, and the rider and longeur can work together on their collective vocabulary. That is to say, the longeur can explain the exercises and the rider can execute them without worrying about the added complication of walking, trotting, or cantering.

A good longeing horse will stand rock solid, all four feet planted on the ground with only an occasional swish of the tail, while his rider does all kinds of contortions in the saddle. Some horses will cock a hoof and drop a hip in a resting position, but should this happen, the longeur can ask the horse to step into a square stance. Encourage the horse, with a gentle cluck or a little action with the whip, to stand on all four legs. Why? If a horse is resting a hip, the rider won't be able to sense that "square and centered" feeling so key to good riding. It's a pretty simple concept—the horse should be standing square because it's easier for the rider to feel if she's balanced and evenly weighting both stirrups, hips, and seat bones. On a horse that chooses to rest his hoof and hip, the rider will feel as if she's sitting on a chair with three good legs and one short one (which is essentially true). It's okay for the horse to snooze while he's standing still as long as all four feet are on the ground.

As you work on the exercises in this book, the longeur changes position accordingly. In the standstill exercises, the longeur stands at the horse's shoulder. At walk, trot, and canter the longeur works at the point of a triangle formed between the horse's shoulder, his hindquarters, and the end of the longe line. Always use proper longeing technique for the best response.

Note that horses who aren't used to standing for a long time might get a little impatient if you've been working for a while without moving. If that's the case, it's no use fighting them; training to stand at the halt happens in another environment without a rider aboard. And although every time you handle a horse you are training it in some way, the longeing sessions in this book are rider-focused. So choose another moment to train the horse to stand still under saddle and on the longe line. Move on to working at the walk, or ask the horse to walk a circle or two before returning to the halt.

To form the circle from the standstill when you're standing at the horse's shoulder, ask the horse to step out and away from you, forming a triangle with his shoulder and hindquarter on either side of you. If you end up in front of his shoulder, he may turn and face you; if you end up behind his hindquarters he may feel he's being chased and quicken his pace. You can vary your position—or angle—to suit your needs. If the horse does begin to turn toward you, step back toward his hindquarters and yield him out on the circle. A well-trained longe horse will respond to a gentle toss of the line or a wave of the whip at his shoulder to send him to a larger circle. The triangle position is a neutral, non-threatening place from which the ground person can control the horse correctly.

To longe in a round circle, pretend you are standing on a manhole cover. You should never step off that imaginary disk; instead, pivot around it on your inside heel. Keep your eyes focused on the rider, which will prevent you from getting dizzy. If you end up walking too much to keep the horse going, he's likely not listening to your cues. Ask the rider to help by adding leg aids to the voice commands to tune the horse in and make him more responsive. Use the whip only as an aid, never as a punishment. Use it low and on the ground behind the hindquarters to encourage the horse forward. If he doesn't listen, bring the whip to mid-waist level, positioning yourself a little behind the shoulder point to drive the horse forward. Try not to lean your body at the horse. Instead remain tall and upright, with your elbows bent yet soft, just as if you were riding. Once the horse is moving nicely, slide the whip into a resting position under your arm pointed away from the horse.

After a few circles of walk, you might be able to bring the horse back to the halt and have him stand quietly. The solid horse will remain unfazed by the rider's waving arms and moving body. And as I noted in Chapter 1, the perfect longe horse should be thoroughly evaluated before a rider on the longe starts flailing around on his back. Still, even the calmest horses can have a moment when something happening above and behind their heads terrifies them. The flight instinct may make him imagine a giant eagle sweeping down to scoop him up in his talons (if horses can imagine such things). So the rider moves quietly first, and if the horse continues standing, the rider can then move with more vigor. I repeat: safety first.

The longeur, meanwhile, can either take her place in the center of the circle, longe line rolled out about twenty feet, or stand at the horse's shoulder. The horse should be facing forward on the circle line. Don't let the horse turn and look at the longeur. If the longeur needs to see what's happening on the other side of the horse, she can switch sides at the shoulder or wait to change direction. And, a skilled longeur can walk to the back of the horse by closing the angle between the horse's hip and the longe line, gradually walking behind the horse as if he were harnessed and she were in the driver's seat of a carriage, to see that the rider is correctly aligned. Remember, though, that in a herd an aggressive movement from behind is often the signal alpha horses use to boss the beta members around. The horse may move forward as you move toward his hindquarters. If this happens, give the whoa signal and go back to your proper place at the apex of the triangle.

During the halt, the longeur suggests exercises, observes they are performed carefully and safely, keeps an eye on the horse and keeps him still, and corrects any unevenness or other incorrect positioning in the rider. This is also the time for the rider and the longeur to establish sequences for each exercise. For example, the rider and longeur can choreograph arm exercises in which the rider places her arms forward toward the horse's ears, then out to the side, then over her head, followed by behind her back (for more ideas on sequence, see page 46). She can use this time to develop her method for moving into and out of each movement, and practice the more complicated exercises that we'll later do at walk, trot, and canter so that the rider gets a feel for them.

Consider this chapter the foundation of the rest of the work in this book. Practice the exercises correctly at the halt and they will be much easier for the rider when the horse is bouncing around at the trot. Practicing each sequence of exercises at the halt will also develop the rider's muscle memory so she won't have to fumble around to find the right position. The two of you can refine the stretch of the arms so when the rider trots with her arms out to the side, for example, she'll remember to keep her muscles taut. When you've practiced at the halt, doing the exercises at the trot and canter isn't a big deal. That builds comfort and confidence in the saddle, allowing the rider to push herself a little more than ordinary.

Master these moves, practice them often, and should the horse spook suddenly on the trail, blast out of the gate toward the barrels, or leave long at a jump, the well-prepared rider stays with him, and—lucky for the horse —does so gently and with a bit of grace. The masters of any equestrian discipline teach you that kindness to the horse in the form of gentle and effective aids is paramount to mastery of the equestrian arts.

The other goal of working at the halt is to build in the rider a sense of her positional faults and how to fix them. A riding instructor shouts, "Left shoulder is drooping" (as I heard so many times and still do now and then) and the rider, who's learned from longe sessions how it feels to have level shoulders, should be able to fix them because the rider and her longeing partner have worked it out. Standstill work allows the rider and the longeur to analyze the rider's position. It allows the team to manipulate exercises and sequences that address those equitation problems without worrying about what the horse is doing. The rider can focus intensely on straightness and re-enact it whenever the longeur notes that the rider is falling into a bad habit.

The third purpose of work at the standstill is comfort. So many adult riders arrive at the sport late—when they finally have the money and time—so they actually don't have those childhood memories of flying down the dirt road galloping or bareback across the pasture. Many of us grow out of fearlessness because we've fallen off a few times, or we're older, or we know how a hospital bill can ruin us. And many of us never had fearlessness to begin with. While some adults who learn to ride in their forties or later may love to ride and love horses, they may approach it with more fear, tightness, and stiffness than younger riders. A rider who becomes comfortable doing a lot of things in the saddle on the longe line when the horse is not moving naturally develops a more secure seat, becoming a more comfortable rider when he is moving. Such ease equals less fear, and less fear equals less stiffness—all of which lead to a better, more enjoyable ride. So practice these exercises sincerely and carefully, stretching to your fullest (without overstretching or hurting yourself), and fool around with different movements. You may even practice dismounting and remounting, if the fear begins when the rider gets on the horse. Whatever feels good.

We do many of these standstill and walk exercises (in fact, all the exercises at all the gaits) with our eyes closed to develop a better sense of feel. With all the instruction in the world, we rarely take the time to focus on our horses beneath us and enjoy the feeling of being on horseback, straight and tall and confident. I know plenty of riders (myself included) who spend hours looking down at their horses' necks while riding; it's as if they turned their gaze away for a moment, the horse would bolt off or disappear from underneath them. The horse isn't going anywhere (most of the time). Think of all the gorgeous scenery riders miss by looking down. We practice these exercises with eyes closed, however, so riders learn to feel confident riding without looking at their horses, the ground, or the planets. They learn to feel.

And don't forget to think of these standstill exercises a bit like the early days of a dance class. Dancers first learn the footsteps, then the arm movements, then what to do with their bodies, and then the embellishments. Then they put it all together. So, too, must riders and longeurs learn the first steps before adding to the exercises. We learn to sit, to sit straighter and taller, to balance without the use of our reins, to change positions without becoming unseated, and to do so at all the different gaits. Pretty soon, we've got that elusive feeling of partnership with our horses.

Squaring Up

This exercise is the basis for everything we'll do on the longe line. It's simple. The horse is standing square. The rider drops her stirrups, letting her legs hang down softly. She lets her arms drop to her sides and her shoulders droop. The rider allows her shoulders to slump forward and the head to drop. She breathes out deeply, letting the air leave all corners and edges of her body. Then she slowly inhales, filling her stomach and then her lungs with air, opening her chest, spreading her arms out to the side

The horse and rider are both square. Note the longeur is standing by the horse's head in this case, asking him to stay still.

and lifting her head to the sky. Then the rider relaxes again by exhaling. Her arms drop to the sides, but she continues to sit tall, and feel her seat bones pressing and thus gently *connecting* to the saddle. The rider feels that her shoulders are level and even, her spine is straight, pelvis slightly tucked, with an open chest and closed eyes.

Sometimes the rider may think she's sitting square but really she's not—perhaps she's collapsing one side of her chest or she's leaning forward. Here the longeur can correct her by pointing out the crookedness. A lot of us have postural habits of which we're not even aware. Such automatic responses become evident when we're asked to sit straight, and even though we think we're sitting erect and even, we're not. Once the longeur has corrected the rider's posture, the longeur can direct the rider to gather all these feelings together and memorize them—*this* is what it feels like to sit straight and square in the saddle.

Stepping Off

For the longeur, the squaring up exercise only requires that the horse remain still. She may even choose to abandon her station at the apex of the triangle and stand next to the horse's shoulder or head, as I mentioned earlier, especially when dealing with a fidgety horse or a rider who feels afraid to close her eyes. Being in close proximity to the rider offers comfort. Assure your rider that you're in control of the horse, he's good (because he passed the longeing test), and he won't go anywhere anyway.

Ask the rider to tilt a tiny bit to the left, staying in that position for a second or two. There are two ways to do so: the first is to ask the rider to weight her left stirrup more than her right one. Or you may ask her to lean left, putting more weight into her left seat bone. Next she can switch sides. Be prepared for the horse to shift his weight. He's feeling the change in the rider's balance. If the rider is insecure about moving in the saddle with her eyes closed, rest one hand gently on her leg just to assure her of your presence and control. Then, with the eyes still closed, ask her to sit straight in the saddle again.

Check your rider:
- Is she straight?
- Shoulders square?
- Seat bones planted on the saddle?
- Hips in line with the horse's shoulders?
- Good posture, with not too much arch in the back?

Adjust any crookedness, and once she is straight again, ask her to raise both arms in the air, reaching toward the clouds. Then have her reach down and put one hand on her center—just below her navel. Hold this position for several breaths and have the rider feel her center. She can switch hands, placing her right hand in the air and her left on her stomach with each deep inhalation, moving her hands slowly with her inhales and exhales.

Although it's hard to see clearly from the ground, note how the rider's body is tilting off to one side for the stepping off exercise.

Advanced Stepping Off

At this point she's learned the exercise, so the rider can move more dramatically. This time, with eyes open, ask her to step deeply into the right stirrup, almost as if she's going to dismount, and lean all the way over. Then try the same exercise on the left side, stepping down into the left stirrup while lightening the weight in the right stirrup. Once the rider has leaned one way and then the other, ask her to sit again in the center of the saddle, lining up the zipper of her breeches or jeans with the pommel or horn of the saddle. Have the rider feel both seat bones square on the saddle with her shoulders and hips even. Essentially she's fixing her own position. Sometimes it helps a slouching or crooked rider to visualize her favorite equestrian—and then imitate that person's position.

I'll reiterate that in the squaring up exercise it's important that the horse is standing evenly on all four feet. A rider that is uneven or unbalanced encourages the horse to be so as well. If the horse shifts his weight to compensate for the rider's position, the longeur is responsible for putting the horse square once again, by using a light touch on the shoulder or slight cue to step forward.

RIDING BLIND

Most often it's very analytical people, those people who like to control the details of their lives, who have a hard time learning to ride. Instead of allowing themselves to feel the clip-clop rhythm of a horse's walk, feel the timing of the canter depart, or just enjoy a nice walk in the woods, they want to know what to do at each step. Learning to ride is frequently about taking steps: first do this, followed by that, as if students are following a recipe. Instructors shout a litany of positional corrections from the edge of the ring: "Heels down! Eyes up!" Meanwhile, some riders need to know the exact "why" behind every movement. But although there certainly are riding recipes, good riders grow beyond the shouted list of instructions and develop an innate sense of the horse and their relationship to it, which makes them truly good horsewomen and men. Longeing, and especially longeing with one's eyes closed, may be nerve-racking for some, but it can help even the tightest rider learn to ride with feel.

Ask the rider to do the same stepping off exercise with her eyes closed this time. Most riders won't want to step as far off—they can't see and therefore believe they can't control what's happening to them. This sensation of loss of control isn't bad, really, because it's something from which we can learn. I've had riders tell me that their fear of closing their eyes manifests itself in motion sickness (especially at the walk and the trot). I offer this gentle reminder to riders who fear the dark. People ski blind, they ride blind, they even play basketball blind. And that is exactly the point of closing the eyes: to mimic what happens naturally to the blind whose other senses develop more strongly to compensate for their loss of vision.

Developing Further Feel

While your rider is sitting squarely with her eyes closed, ask her to describe what she's feeling both from an emotional and physical standpoint. Ask for a little free association (the first words that come into her head). Words that may come to mind include *insecure*, *fearful*, *tight*, *gripping*, or "just fine, thank you." Her response may be physical (pain, soreness, or tightness) or it may be emotional. A part of her body may be aching, or she may feel uneven. If it's a physical tightness, ask her to try an exercise that's prescribed for insomniacs and those who wish to learn to meditate. Ask the rider to intensely flex and relax each part of her body in sequence working up from her toes. She can tense and relax all the way to her head. Afterwards, she'll be relaxed and centered. Ask again for her to describe how each part of her body is feeling. This exercise builds relaxed body awareness—most of riding is, after all, finding ways to physically sync up your body with your horse's movement—actions that can't be "thought" but rather must be felt.

If the rider is too frightened to keep her eyes closed, have her try small increments—just a few seconds at a time. Deep breathing can accompany closed eyes. The deep breathing technique I like is based on a four-count inhale, four-count exhale deep into the lower stomach. With her eyes closed, the rider breathes for one cycle of four. For the next breath she opens her eyes. Gradually add a cycle of four so she keeps her eyes closed for eight counts and open for four. The focus on breathing takes her mind off her fear. And it's no surprise: deep breathing has been practiced for centuries as a relaxation exercise. After you've worked on relaxation and breathing, try stepping off with eyes closed again, to see if it feels any more comfortable to the rider.

Soft Gaze

After she's closed her eyes for a while, ask her to open the eyes with just a soft gaze. Yogis call this focusing on the third eye—a spot in the middle of your forehead just above the eyebrow line. Of course if you did actually *look* at this spot you'd be cross-eyed and give yourself a headache, so instead the rider can just imagine the spot where the third eye would be. By focusing on an imaginary point, you can actually widen your field of vision. We know the old instructor's saying: "Keep your eyes up." When you ride you're supposed to focus on a point ahead of you. Instead of looking at a tree, a bush, or the next point in the arena, ask the rider to open her gaze to incorporate her peripheral vision. Opening the gaze encourages relaxation. When you're actually riding, you need to focus on the line of travel—such as a cow coming out of the chute, the next jump, or the circle line in dressage, but for now you're just focused on relaxation. After the rider has identified and practiced the soft gaze, she can try it two or three times, alternating between the hard, focused eye and the soft one. Your rider should quickly become erect, centered, and relaxed.

LEGS AND FEET

In riding, we're sometimes asked to perform the equivalent of patting our stomachs and rubbing our heads at the same. Indeed, riding is a series of co-ordinated movements between the arms, legs, and bodies of both horse and rider. And sometimes we're using cues that oppose our natural instincts—we have to learn to be ambidextrous with feet and hands. No one, horse or human, moves with perfect symmetry, but that's our goal. Riding is one of the few sports that demand we learn to use both sides of our bodies with equal strength and agility. Soccer players, for example, play positions that allow them to use their stronger leg more frequently. Baseball pitchers modify their throws for left-handed batters.

It's not easy to break the body's natural habits, so when we do exercises like the ankle circles we'll practice next on the longe, isolate the movement first. You'll begin by moving each foot individually; then you'll move them together, making circles in the same direction, then you'll move them at the same time but in opposite directions. So there are four phases to every exercise: first one side, then the other side, then both sides together, then both sides moving in opposition.

Ankle Circles

Ask the rider to drop her stirrups and circle her ankles gently. Start with the left ankle, turning the foot in a circle without making contact with the horse. The rider needs to move her leg out and away from the horse's side so she doesn't give him an accidental kick. To turn the foot in a circle, first the rider points her toe up, then to the outside, then down to the ground, then toward the horse's flank.

Some riders have more ankle mobility than others—riders with tight calf muscles might have to work a little harder at this stretch. It loosens the

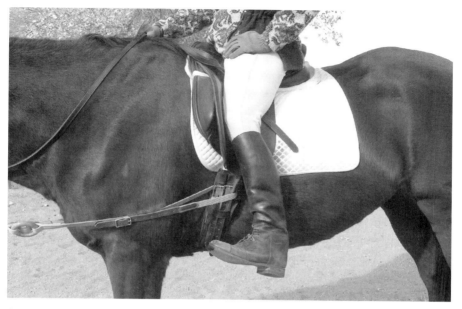

Some riders have more mobility in their ankles than others. Here, the beginning stage of ankle circles.

legs and helps the rider to manipulate her ankles and feet in case she loses her stirrup and must search for it while in motion.

After the rider circles her left ankle clockwise for several circles, have her circle it counterclockwise. Then repeat the exercise on the right side. And, because we are naturally more coordinated on one side or the other (and don't be surprised if the more coordinated foot is actually the opposite of your more coordinated hand), the rider may find this exercise weirdly difficult. We're frequently more coordinated on the left because we so often work with our horses from that side. It's a habit.

Once the rider has practiced the ankle circles on each side separately and then moving the feet together at the same time clockwise, you can confuse her by asking her to circle each foot in opposite directions: left foot clockwise, right foot counterclockwise. Your rider isn't going to master this exercise the first time around. In fact, she may never master it. Her feet will turn every which way, and you may even see your rider do strange things with her wrists—I've seen riders tense their hands when concentrating on their feet. The point of longeing isn't to achieve perfection in each exercise; it's to try to move the body in different ways on horseback so you become comfortable. Encourage your rider to enjoy the hilarity of being uncoordinated.

Foot Flex

Another exercise for times when the rider's feet are out of the stirrups and the horse is at a standstill is the foot flex. The rider points her toes to the ground, flexing the arch of her foot. Point the toes as far down as possible to fully stretch the calf muscles, lengthen the leg, and open the muscles of the thigh. Tense riders tend to grip with their thighs, causing them to "pop" upward and out of the tack.

Try the opposite—point the toes to the sky with heels down. The flex of the heel especially serves riders who like to jump, because they have to carry their weight in their lower legs to remain balanced over fences. For dressage riders and Western riders, a flatter foot is more appropriate, but flexing the feet up and down softens the ankle, which absorbs some of the bounce and allows the rider to sit gently in the saddle.

Have the rider flex each foot several times. Then, as with the ankle circles, ask the

Here the rider flexes her foot up and down to loosen her ankle.

rider to flex both feet in unison, and then in opposite directions—right foot pointing up while the left foot is pointing down. Again, the rider might feel uncoordinated, but I can't emphasize enough that this is all for fun—there is no success or failure, just exploration.

Runner's Stretch

Many of the exercises in this book have been borrowed from other sports or physical practices. Yoga appears frequently, since the centering, calming aspects of this ancient art are in concert with the principles of riding. So, too, do basic stretches from other sports. Even the movements taught in African dance traditions, in which shoulders and hips are moving and flexible but controlled, appear in the exercises.

Runners and cyclists, for example, stretch before heading off on their athletic endeavors. One favorite that translates well to horseback riding is the runner's quadriceps stretch. On the ground, the runner bends one leg behind him and grabs his ankle with his hand on the same side. Note that when runners stretch, they continue to stand straight—they don't overarch their backs, misalign their hips, or lean back. The same concept holds on horseback. The rider remains right in the center of the saddle, and bends her left knee so the leg folds with the ankle toward the back of her thigh. She grabs

A variation on the runner's stretch for a less limber rider. Note the straight spine.

the ankle without overarching her spine. Some less flexible riders may not be able to reach their ankles without overarching. Such a rider bends her leg from the knee, omitting the ankle grab portion of the exercise. If she is able to grab her ankle, and seems flexible enough, have her press from the upper thigh down through the knee to open her hip flexor, so she feels she's stretching her knee to the ground. Hold the position for fifteen seconds, and then release. Repeat on the opposite side, and then, if your rider is feeling loose and not overarching her back, have her try the runner's stretch with both legs at the same time.

Sally Swift, author of *Centered Riding*, uses a visualization called "stubby legs" to help riders understand proper leg positioning—basically the knee is pointed down to the ground and the lower leg is soft until it is needed as an aid. The runner's stretch is exactly the type of exercise you can use to help the rider visualize and actualize Swift's concept: because the lower leg is behind you, out of contact with the horse, the upper leg is in a very good riding position, knees pointing downward, thighs open and stretched. When the rider has both legs in runner's stretch, the longeur assures the rider isn't either tilting forward off her hipbones or tilting backward behind the vertical line from the spine to the ground. Most importantly, the rider's back should be flat and not overarched.

Make sure to practice runner's stretch on both sides for the same amount of time. Don't be surprised if one thigh is tighter than the other.

Bicycle

The goal of the bicycle exercise is to have the upper body remain on the centered upright line, while moving the legs independently. The bicycle is an especially good exercise to practice if you find the sitting trot too jarring to tolerate, or if your back stiffens, or you find yourself unbalanced. We'll practice it at the halt briefly so the rider will have the feel of it when she's ready to practice it at the trot.

Start sitting straight and centered. Have the rider lift alternating knees toward her chest as if pedaling a bicycle that is too small for her. The action should come from the hips but especially the lower abdomen; the upper body should stay as still as possible. The longeur counts out a one-two-three-four beat. It should take four beats to move each leg. Once you get to trotting, the rider will greatly accelerate the motion to keep up with the horse's trot pace, but at the standstill we're working only on learning the movement of the exercise before we speed it up.

The opposite of the runner's stretch is the bicycle. The rider lifts alternating knees up and down while remaining centered with her torso and hips.

Here are a few items the longeur should watch for:

- The rider should stay tall in the saddle while her legs are moving up and down. Some people either lean forward on their crotch or lean back—the rider should feel an imaginary pole through her spine down to the ground to keep her hips lined up with the horse's shoulders and her own shoulders in line with her hips. No forward or backward tilting.

- Make sure the rider is keeping her heels down and leg long on the downward part of the exercise. Otherwise she's likely to accidentally jam the patient horse into gear. With a flat foot and a long leg, she can get the feeling of stepping on the ground with each movement.

- The arms can either be hanging gently by the rider's sides in imaginary rein position or, if it helps, the rider can put her hands on her center, on the bucking strap, or on the saddle to help stabilize her upper body. Pretending there are reins helps the rider prepare for how it would feel to do this exercise at the trot. It also reminds the rider to keep her shoulders still.

- The legs and the arms sometimes want to move together—a neuromuscular attachment that's hard to break. As the rider's legs move, the arms should stay quiet, however; no clenched wrists or flailing shoulders, no movement in the upper body. Only the rider's legs should move.

UPPER BODY

Now we'll work a little on the shoulders—moving them around to loosen up and release any rider tension or stiffness. These exercises also help to rid the rider of slouching. It's a lot easier to wiggle the shoulders around at a standstill than when the horse is moving. Later we'll repeat these movements at the walk and trot, where the rider will need to think about the rhythm of the movement while at the same time moving her arms and shoulders freely.

Tighten-and-Release

A good way to loosen tight shoulders (and any other part of the body) is what I call the tighten-and-release method. This pulsing action frees muscle constriction. It also illustrates the difference between tension and relaxation. For example, as the rider raises her right arm high over her head, she stretches it to the sky as if climbing or grabbing the clouds, tightening all the muscles in her arm and straightening the elbow—that's the tight part of the exercise. In part two, the rider, while keeping her arm skyward, releases the flex, softening the muscles but maintaining enough tension to hold the arm up. The tighten-and-release helps the muscles stretch. It builds awareness of the neutral flexed-but-soft muscles where effective riding takes place—the kind of placid control that requires strength, direction, and relaxation all at once. This tighten-and-release technique can apply to all the exercises here. Use the technique to release tension, cope with fear, and build stronger, more energetic muscles. Then do the exercise with the other arm.

Shoulder Rolls

I picked up this exercise in an African dance class. At first, it was difficult for me to separate parts of my body without moving other parts. Watching the other dancers, I noticed the good ones move like marionettes. A string seemed to be attached to the part of the body they were moving. For example, one dancer would move her shoulders right but her hips would stay centered. The teacher frequently kept one hand on her lower stomach to remind herself and the students to keep the lower body solid. The dancers seemed to have a great deal of control over individual parts, which then were able to move as a whole.

In this exercise, I stress exactly the same concept: independent yet whole. A shoulder that can move to the left or to the right without taking the seat bones and hips out of alignment would be useful for your favorite riding discipline—whether that's riding on the trail or jumping a 3'6" course. Whatever happens, you need to be centered, and able to return yourself to center should you get unbalanced.

Begin in our centered and straight posture. The rider imagines a handle placed right in the middle of the sternum. Visualize an imaginary hand pushing on the handle, causing the chest to collapse and the shoulders to slump forward. The back remains in the same position, the hips immobile and the seat like clay—solid but molding to the horse. The shoulders collapse around the center point of the sternum, then straighten up again. Repeat that four times, and then reverse the action, so the imaginary hand is pulling the handle out and the shoulders are coming back, shoulder blades squeezing together. The longeur can ask the rider to hug an imaginary pencil resting vertically down her spine and between her shoulder blades with each repetition of squeezing. This will release any tightness in front of the chest, open the sternum, and give the rider the feeling of having her shoulders back. The longeur can add rhythm to the exercise by guiding the rider's repetition; the longeur counts to eight for shoulders forward and then eight for shoulders back.

Part two of this series requires the rider to visualize a long pole from the top of her head down her spine, dissecting the horse and reaching the ground. Using only the sternum, the rider shifts her rib cage to the right, keeping the imaginary pole exactly even between the hips and through the horse's spine. Then she shifts the rib cage to the left. Repeat each direction four times, remembering to use four count breaths along the way. Once the rider has established the movement, the longeur can make sure the rider's sternum and shoulders are mobile enough to loosen her lower back and flex the shoulders, alleviating tension in her upper back.

The rider should stretch tall in the saddle in between exercises to remove kinks or tight spots that may have developed in her spine, particularly in her lower back. It also helps to improve the rider's muscle memory of what "straight" feels like. Many riders struggle to maintain a correct position. Riders get busy trying to fix their horses or looking at the trail or concentrating on something totally unrelated to riding. Lo and behold, they're slumping, or twisting, or reverting to an old riding habit. The idea of returning to center is a tool the rider can use whenever she senses she's crooked. Use the in-between exercises—centering, sitting straight, and breathing—to realign the rider's body to that straight-as-a-pole-but-soft-as-clay feeling.

Cat-Cow

If you've studied yoga, you may recognize "cat-cow" as a rough English translation of a Sanskrit word for a traditional yoga pose. On horseback, cat-cow can help the rider release tension in the lower spine. It is particularly good for riders who tend to overarch their backs or carry tension in their shoulders. It can also help riders understand the feeling of sliding the pelvis underneath themselves, helping them to flatten an overarched spine. As the longeur, emphasize to the rider the feeling of moving each vertebra individually.

Cat-cow. Here Michelle has a very strong arch to her back in both positions.

To practice cat-cow on the ground, kneel down on hands and knees, and gently arch your back, one vertebra at a time, rolling up your spine until you are lifting the bones in the neck; then reverse the process, slowly bringing your back up and dropping your head like an angry cat.

Here's how you do it on horseback: Have the rider lean forward and place a hand on each of the horse's shoulder blades or on the sides of his neck. There should be a few inches between the rider's belly and the horn or pommel of the saddle. The rider starts in a natural, leaning forward position, pressing one vertebra at a time toward the horse, starting from the lower back and working up toward the neck until her back is arched like a swaybacked cow. Once she's fully arched, she slowly drops her head and reverses the arch, again emphasizing slowness and awareness of the spine, to the angry cat position. Repeat this exercise five times and remind the rider to go slowly and concentrate on the bones in her spine. Incorporate four-count breathing to help the rider get a full stretch: inhale four counts into the arch, and exhale four counts into the opposite position.

THE TOP: FUN WITH SPINNING

A summer camp pony named Doodles was a tolerant soul, never flicking an ear while we pretended he was a circus pony. We stood on his back, rode him backwards, and taught ourselves to somersault off him. One of the more fun and less risky Doodles tricks followed me to this book. I tried it with an adult beginner student recently after we spent an intense fifteen minutes working on the trot posting diagonal. She felt her brain might explode, so instead we stopped, took a breath and did "the top," also known as Around the World.

The top can be done as slowly or as quickly as the rider feels comfortable doing it. The longeur's job is simply to hold the horse steady and quiet; if the rider needs reassurance, the longeur may put one hand on the rider's leg or lightly on her waist. The purpose is just plain fun—to reclaim a bit of that girls-playing-pony-in-the-circus feeling, to release tension, and to learn that horses aren't scary and that you can do quite a lot on their backs without them caring.

Have the rider put one hand on the cantle and the other on the horn or the pommel. The rider should twist in the saddle and gradually bring her right leg up and over the horse's neck, so both legs are on the left side of the horse. From here the rider could just slide off and land on both feet, facing away from the horse. Instead, though, the rider can slide a little back in the saddle toward the right side of the horse. Next have her swing her left leg over the horse's rump to the right side. The rider is now facing backwards.

Samantha (age twelve) frequently rides her pony Domino backwards, sideways, and for-wards. She's happy to demonstrate around the world.

Next she brings her right leg over the rump so she has both legs on the right side of the horse, and then she brings the left leg over the horn or pommel again so she's facing front. The rider can repeat this exercise three times and also reverse it, with her first move to the right side of the horse instead of the left. Think of this exercise as lubricating the rider's hip flexors as well as stimulating her fun meter.

The rider and the longeur may not feel like they're accomplishing much working these exercises at a dead halt, but you'll be building up the basis for the work that happens later on this book, and in your riding life.

A word about the sequences we've included at the end of each chapter: they are meant only as suggestions—the longeur and rider can choreograph a series of exercises to suit individual problems, needs, and positional struggles.

Series A
Shoulder slump and straighten
(four times)
Arms over head and back to
sides (four times)
Four count breaths

Series B
Toe circles (both ankles, four
rotations)
Bicycle (one pedal push)

Series C
Bicycle (four times)
Arms over head (hold for four
seconds)
Combine arms overhead/bicycle
with legs

Series D
Arms overhead
Stepping off right
Arms overhead
Stepping off left

Chapter 3
WALK

An instructor used to say to me, "If he was going any slower he'd be going backwards." That's not the kind of walk we want here. For this series, the horse needs to be really walking. Not ambling, not poking along, not "nearly stopping." We want a marching horse, stomping along in a clear one-two-three-four rhythm. Not fast, but forward. What's the difference? The forward walk maintains the rhythm established by the longeur or the rider. The hooves fall in this order: left fore, right hind, right fore, left hind. When the horse gets tense, he can feel like he's pacing. Although some gaited horses have this trait as part of their breeding, otherwise it is a sign the walk is tense and too fast. Instead of the one-two-three-four rhythm, it will feel more like one-two . . . three-four. Sometimes you hear this referred to as a lateral walk because instead of diagonal pairs moving in sequence, same-side pairs move in sequence: left fore and hind, right fore and hind.

The longeur regulates the walk pace and maintains the gait. Even before the rider begins the exercises, the longeur establishes the walk rhythm by asking the horse to step away from her position and toward the outside of the circle, using two rotations to reach the full extension of the longe line. Along the way, the longeur and rider can build the horse's step into a forward, marching walk. The rider remains soft, "following" the horse's movements with her seat. Often "following" can be mistaken for a pushing or pumping movement with the hips. If the rider is moving too much, remind her to relax and follow, using breathing exercises to move the concentration from her hips and seat to her center. The concentration on breathing in time to the walk will improve the quality and arrest the pumping motion, which can actually cause the horse to tighten and lose his natural rhythm. The ideal walk is the naturally forward rhythm of a regular horse coming in from the pasture for dinner (and not a starving, excited horse who hears the sound of the feed cart and comes galloping). Imagine what a herd looks like as it's moving actively toward food. That's the feeling we want to achieve with the walk.

If your equine longeing partner still feels tight, it's time for some troubleshooting. If the horse is a normally well-behaved forward-walking fellow who appears tense, jiggy, or otherwise unhappy, the longeur has the responsibility of analyzing what's wrong. A series of questions can help the rider identify parts of her body that might be working against overall relaxation.

Take a rider inventory by asking her these questions:

- Are your legs relaxed and long, with the ball of each foot resting gently on the stirrup bars without pushing them out in front of you?

- Are your thighs open and loose?

- Are your hips following gently, but not pushing?

- Are your seat bones soft but in contact with the horse's back? Can you feel the horse moving through your seat or are you somehow resisting his movement?

- Perhaps there's something blocked in your lower back? Are you allowing the area from your sacrum—the flat disk at the base of your spine—to your fourth or fifth vertebrae, to remain fluid?

- Are your arms hanging gently at your sides with your shoulder blades soft and rolling downwards?

If the answer to most of these questions is yes, either your rider is terribly un-self-aware, or you need to switch horses. If you've chosen your longeing mount correctly and your rider can identify some tight places, you should see a change in the horse once the rider sits up tall, relaxes her seat bones and gluteus muscles, and follows more actively with her hips. Most commonly, you'll find that the tense rider is squeezing her butt cheeks together. For the horse, it feels a bit like having a paperclip on either side of his spine. There is a relationship between the rider's concentration level and the tightness of her gluteus maximus. The more concentrated the rider, the more she risks inadvertently pinching, and the more pinching there is the more tension there will be in both the rider and the horse. So remember that visual of keeping the rider's hindquarters soft, firm, but moldable.

Any exercise the rider does at the standstill can be repeated at the walk, even "the top" from the previous chapter. Even if the horse is very quiet and the rider has a horn or bucking strap to hold, it takes a balanced rider to sit sideways, backwards, sideways, and forward while the horse is walking. This is one exercise at the walk where the longeur, for safety's sake, wouldn't be at the point of the triangle between the horse's shoulder and hindquarters. If you do choose to try this exercise, the longeur should remain close to the horse's shoulder to serve as the rider's spotter.

Once the horse has moved out on his circle and the longeur has paid out the longe line—making a circle that's forty to sixty feet in diameter (at full extension of a thirty-foot longe line)—the longeur can slow the walk by squeezing her hand on the line and using a soft "whoa" voice command. To activate the walk so the horse's hind hooves step lively into his front hooves' tracks, extend your longeing hand just a little to soften the contact with the bit, and raise your whip slightly. A voice command said in the rhythm you want the horse to mimic helps, depending on how attuned the horse is to the longeur. It would go like this: "Walk-ing, walk-ing, walk-ing" (separating the syllables so two "walk-ings" makes four beats). Clucking works well, too. Once the horse finds the rhythm, you should be able to leave him alone and concentrate on the rider.

Now that the horse is moving, we can try the exercises. The rider should also be feeling more comfortable, since she's been standing quietly for a long time. Even the timid rider might be able to perform some of the same exercises at the walk that she did during the standstill. That's the best way to start walk work—review what you've already done at the halt. Later in this chapter I'll incorporate the walk rhythm.

Change directions frequently when working at the walk. Despite the fact that our bodies appear symmetrical—two arms, two legs, two eyes, two ears, and one nose right down the middle—no one actually is. Most riders have been through the vagaries of life—skiing accidents, car wrecks, too many hours in front of a keyboard with their right leg crossed over their left leg—whatever the situation, the adult body is going to be uneven. And an adult with an uneven body who regularly rides the same horse will cause similar unevenness in her equine partner. That's why it's important to change directions frequently, and why we do every exercise on both sides with both legs and arms.

Always begin your walk longeing session by questioning the rider about her riding struggles. Say, for example, your rider has been feeling like she can't find an even stirrup length—perhaps one leg needs to be stretched or moved. Here's where you can combine certain sequences to release the muscle tightness that may be causing the leg to contract at the knee or slip back out of position. Experiment and vary the series—spinning wrists, arm circles, helicopters, leg fluffs, and so forth in any order or with any timing that feels right.

UPPER BODY

Arm Circles

Begin with the rider's feet in the stirrups. Have the rider extend her arms out to the sides, stretching to the fingertips. She can concentrate on keeping her arms taut—no wimpy elbows or muscles.

In this position, the rider makes slow circles (with both arms) in rhythm with the horse's walk. With each hoofbeat, have the rider move her arms a quarter of a circle. Complete two circles and then reverse the direction of the arms. If she started in a clockwise direction, reverse to a counterclockwise direction.

The longeur reminds the rider to keep moving her arms but also to keep them stretched with energy all the way from the

Taut arms stretched out to the side and a straight body center the rider over the horse correctly at the walk.

Variations on arm exercises: stretched up and in front. All three positions work the kinks out of the rider's upper back and shoulders.

shoulders to the fingertips. Complete two circles while moving the arms forward, and then two backward. Then ask the rider to shake out her arms, loosen the shoulders, and relax for a moment.

For a variation on this theme, have the rider stretch her arms in front of her, then out to the side, then over her head following the walk rhythm. Keep each movement to two counts—arms front, one-two; arms side, one-two; arms up, one-two; arms in rein position, one-two. Moving quickly between different postures builds coordination.

Clasped Arms

The next movement opens the upper body and loosens tightness in the shoulders. Have the rider reach back behind her and clasp her hands together while straightening her arms. Remind her to squeeze her shoulder blades together tightly. This will improve the openness in the sternum, lift the chest, and stretch the front of the shoulders and rotator cuffs. This exercise doesn't have to be performed in walk rhythm since it's static. If the rider wants to deepen the stretch she can squeeze and release her shoulder blades. The longeur needs to pay attention to the rider's head, held upright and not tilting forward or otherwise falling off her "center pole." It's tempting to fall or lean forward to raise the arms up higher, but it's better to have less stretch than to lose the centered body. The rider should try to get as much stretch as possible in the arms. A gentle pulsing motion is one way to achieve this—just a half inch of upward pulsing might bring the arms into a deeper stretch.

With the arms stretched out and hands clasped behind the rider, ask her to swivel the torso right and left, now using the rhythm of the horse's walk—one-two (to the right), one-two (to the left). The longeur should make sure the rider's hips stay in line with the horse's shoulders and hindquarters. While the torso swivels, the hips remain pointing straight forward. After two circles, the rider can release her clasped hands, relax her shoulders, and shake her arms out to loosen up.

A favorite for riders who spend more time in front of the computer than in the saddle, the rider squeezes her shoulder blades together, opens her chest, and clasps her hands behind her back.

The rider can repeat the exercise with the arms in the front—hands clasped together with index fingers pointing toward the horse's ears. Keep the arms stretched taut, using the rhythm of the horse's walk to swivel the upper body right and left, first counting two beats right and then two beats left. The hips remain squarely in line with the horse's body.

Moving the upper body while keeping hips and legs in alignment gives the rider the feeling of being centered, while having mobility in her torso. It reminds the rider that the arms and upper torso can swivel while the legs and the hips remain still. An important benefit is to open the rider's shoulders and stretch through tension she might be experiencing in her shoulders.

Wrists

To build coordination, have the rider hold her arms out to the side again, stretching the arm muscles fully. Ask her to bend the left wrist, pointing the fingertips down to the ground, and bend the right wrist up, pointing fingers to the sky. Physiologist Eckhart Meyners, who works with international dressage riders, notes that cross-coordination helps the rider manage the diagonal aids more effectively. Asking the body to work in opposition builds neuromuscular coordination since it breaks the body's normal movement habits.

You can do these oppositional exercises for any two parts of the body. Rotate your left wrist in a clockwise circle while moving the right counterclockwise; circle your left foot clockwise while moving your right wrist counterclockwise. Swivel your left lower leg one way and right lower leg the other. This does take concentration. Ultimately, these exercises force the body to think. Sometimes we develop riding habits, such as always having a bouncing right hand or a twist in the upper body. One rider I know bends her wrists and tenses her arms when she's concentrating. Another presses her tongue against her lower lip, causing a lump. Working in opposition, such as twisting the wrists in opposite directions, helps to break body habits and reminds us that we can move in other ways than we're accustomed to.

As the horse is walking briskly forward as if marching toward that imaginary food bin, the longeur asks the rider to circle each wrist individually in a clockwise direction. Next the rider can rotate both wrists at the same time in the same direction. Remind the rider to keep her eyes forward, guiding the horse around the circle line in advance of the horse's footfalls. Remind the rider, too, to keep her arms taut and out to the side. Take a break after two circles to shake out the arms. Rest the arms for a circle, and then repeat the exercise.

Now you can combine the wrist circles with timing. Ask the rider to perform each part of this exercise for four counts. Point the fingers up (bending at the wrist); point them down; and circle them in the same direction. Once you've circled the hands and wrists the same way at the same

Moving the wrists and hand in opposite directions builds coordination.

time, ask the rider to circle the hands in opposite direction at the same time for four counts. Then ask the rider to add arm circles into the sequence: circling the arms same direction for four counts of the walk, and then in opposite directions. You can continue tacking on variations as the rider becomes proficient.

THE LEGS

When we're riding, our legs form the engine, our accelerator, and our roots to the ground. Flexibility and the ability to move our legs independently are essential to being a good rider, whether you're out on the trail or in the arena, jumping or practicing dressage. Depending on your skill, your legs are either going to help or hinder your riding. The left and right legs should move by themselves. Each part of the leg should move as the rider asks it to. For example, if you move your left leg slightly back to ask your horse to canter, your left hip stays in place. Your right leg, too, shouldn't move just because your left leg does. If you want to practice a half pass in dressage, the left leg *and* hip open to cue the horse to bend. If you're running barrels, standing up and forward quickly and then sitting back and down quickly will be key to making tight turns and fast gallops. To jump, you have to be able to sink deeply into your knees and heels without kicking your lower leg behind or in front of you.

Stirrups On and Off

To start, work on dropping and finding your stirrups. This exercise demands a little patience, but has many benefits. When you lose a stirrup—which might actually be a sign that one or the other of your legs is pinching, your stirrups are uneven, or you're otherwise unbalanced—knowing how to find your irons again quickly is an undeniably good skill to have. Not everyone can fly over a cross-country course missing a stirrup, or stay balanced on a bouncy dressage horse while one foot is in the stirrup and one is out. Practicing will help.

The rider should take care not to give the horse a kick or squeeze accidentally. The longeur needs to be prepared to correct this common rider fault, while maintaining the horse's marching forward walk rhythm. If the horse speeds up or grows tense while the rider is feeling around for her stirrup, ask her to drop her leg once again and start over.

Some riders just aren't comfortable riding without stirrups. If that's the case, you can do a few of the exercises detailed below with the stirrups, or work more thoroughly on the forthcoming leg fluffs and posting at the walk, and the upper body work we've already done. By no means do I encourage a longeur to push a fearful rider beyond her comfort level. However, the longeur might try asking the rider to drop her stirrups just for one circle, and

Dropping and finding the stirrups prepares the rider for emergencies, builds flexibility for the ankles, and helps her to position her foot correctly: toe up and in, heel down.

then pick them up again, gradually increasing the number of rotations. This is the first step to a more confident rider and it's worth trying. Incremental steps work better than one big push.

As the rider and horse circle, the rider drops both her stirrups and lets her legs hang relaxed. The arms remain passive by the rider's sides, with the shoulders back and the shoulder blades pressing together to lift the sternum. The rider's eyes are focused between the horse's ears. Longe the rider around one complete circle.

One leg at a time, starting with the inside so the longeur can see what that leg is doing, ask the rider to aim her eyes straight ahead (no cheating!), point her toe up, and rotate her heel out a bit. Since the natural position of the stirrup at rest is lying nearly flat against the horse, and the stirrup length is shorter than the rider's leg, she'll have to turn her toe both up and in to find the iron. Not everyone retrieves it on the first try. If the rider really can't find her stirrup she's allowed to look at her foot (but don't allow her to reach for or touch the stirrup leather—the idea here is to develop feel). Once she's found one stirrup she can search around for the other. Practice three more times, dropping the stirrups for one entire circle so the leg stretches long, and then finding them again. Besides being extremely helpful for riders who lose their stirrups while riding, this exercise is important for rider safety. For example, if you're somehow unseated and feel like you may fall off, the most important thing to do immediately is to drop your stirrups so you won't get caught in them and dragged, should you fall off. You'll practice this exercise at each of the three gaits so it's no big deal to remain balanced and find your stirrup again without having to bounce unbalanced back to a walk or halt.

Ankle Circles at the Walk

Once you've practiced picking up and dropping your stirrups, drop them again for the next series of exercises. Letting the legs hang long, ask the rider to point one set of toes up and one set down, mimicking the wrist exercise. Flex one foot and then the other; flex both feet up and then both feet down; and then rotate the ankles. The longeur can watch that the rider isn't accidentally kicking the horse.

Although you can perform these exercises in the walk rhythm, it's best to first focus on coordination and range of motion. If the rider becomes proficient at circling her ankles in opposite directions at the same time, the longeur can add in the four-beat count, asking the rider to move a quarter turn around the ankle circle with each beat. The longeur needs to pay particular attention to whether the rider's ankles are moving enough. A lot of people have limited mobility in their ankles and tend to shortcut the part of the circle where the toe turns in and the heel turns out. While not a crucial movement for riding, it is important to be able to move this way if, for example, you lose a stirrup out on the trail as detailed above.

Loosening up the ankles has an added benefit. It reminds the body that it has mobility below the ankles, and that the feet aren't just for walking. Feet can actually move independently of the walk motion, which builds an awareness of the lower extremities that's necessary for all aspects of riding—from being loose enough to reposition the entire leg to having enough body awareness to curl your pinky toe underneath your fourth toe, a motion that helps to bring the leg flat against the horse's side.

Piano Scales

Working down the foot, the longeur can ask the rider to play piano scales with her toes. The exercise takes the rider's focus away from fear. Obviously the longeur won't be able to see if the rider is doing this correctly, but again, it's a way for the rider to focus on a single, often neglected body part. The longeur has to trust that the rider is, indeed, moving her toes, but the boot remains still. Moving toes around in the boots can have an amazing impact on foot and leg positioning. Sometimes riders tense their toes in the same way they tense their wrists when they're concentrating. Asking the rider to move her toes is a trick to apply when the rider seems particularly tense. Ask her to wiggle her toes and watch the rider's focus shift from fear, or whatever part of the body the rider is concentrating on, to the feet—and you should see a significant change.

To loosen up for the next series, ask the rider to swivel her lower legs from the knees down, without interfering with the horse's flanks. Sometimes it helps to have the rider point her toes down in a ballerina position. The longeur watches for any movement of the upper leg. For now we're isolating each body part in preparation for the next part of the walk sequence.

Scissor Legs

Next we're working on controlling the entire leg without moving the seat bones or unbalancing the area from the hips to the head. The rider will naturally want to fall back behind the vertical line when she moves her legs forward (frequently referred to as a chair seat) or tilt forward when she

Scissor legs, part one, involves flexing one leg intensely forward and backward.

moves her legs behind the vertical (leaning forward with the upper torso). The longeur watches the rider's body to assure she doesn't become unbalanced in her upper section.

Leave the stirrups dangling (later she'll cross them over the horse's neck). Have the rider stretch her legs long; flex the toes, feet, and ankles a few times to loosen up; and shake out the shoulders and the back to release any tightness. The rider flexes her whole inside leg, pointing the toes toward the ground in front of the horse's shoulder. With the leg still flexed and pointed, ask her to move her entire leg, from the hip flexor and not from the knee, behind her hip, so her flexed toes are pointing toward the ground behind the girth, or even further, depending on the rider's flexibility. Many riders never use their hip flexors in this fashion and a muscle cramp might ensue, so don't overdo it. Make sure the rider moves only as far as necessary to feel a stretch, and not to where the muscles and tendons begin to pull. I'd highly recommend a regular practice of stretching and strength training, such as yoga, tai chi, or Pilates, to improve the flexibility of the hips.

If the rider does get a cramp, have her bend forward and lift her knee to her chest. Then have the rider walk a few circles doing whatever feels comfortable at the time to loosen that muscle. She may need to find her stirrups again to relieve pressure from the hip flexor. Although it sounds inevitable that this exercise will be painful, it really isn't—I bring it up only because many people have tight hips and my longeing partner and I have both gotten hip flexor cramps. So have our students.

Scissor legs, with one leg pointed forward and one back, improves hip flexibility.

If the rider is able to, she can stretch the leg back and forward—the first stage of scissor legs. Once she understands how to move from the hip and not from the knee—an important distinction—practice with the other leg. You might want to try this in both directions before moving on to the full scissoring motion so you fix any asymmetry.

The scissor exercise gets its name from the backward and forward motion of the legs in a scissoring action, without the hips moving. The torso, hips, and seat bones follow the horse's walk motion. The rider keeps her knees straight (but not locked) and her toes pointed to the ground as she moves one flexed leg forward and one flexed leg back. She can switch them back and forth, so it looks as if she's walking with straight knees.

To incorporate this exercise into the walk's four-beat rhythm, the longeur watches the horse's hind legs. As the inside hind comes forward, the rider's inside leg should come forward. Tighter riders can switch legs every fourth beat, while more flexible riders can switch legs every second beat, following the action of the horse's hind legs. We'll do some "feel" exercises to develop a rider's sense of the horse's leg movement, but for now the longeur helps the rider identify the legs, saying, "Inside, outside, inside, outside."

Scissoring is a great loosening exercise, and it also develops a strong sense of the horse's motion. Some points to watch for:

- The rider's torso and hips point forward; no swiveling left and right.

- The upper body should stay as quiet as possible. If needed, have the rider place both hands on the bucking strap, or a hand on each side of the horn, or even better, carry the hands in rein position.

- The seat bones and gluteus maximus should be planted, but not rock hard, in the saddle.

Once the rider has scissored her legs, ask her to explore how her body feels, describing the motion and what her hips and legs are doing. Does she feel unbalanced or tight somewhere? It may feel completely awkward. It's important the rider feel that her hips are centered while her legs do separate motions. The purpose of longeing is to build body awareness and a better feel for the horse, so simply performing the exercises won't help the rider unless she actually can verbalize how her body feels. Better yet, she can close her eyes and breathe in those sensations, trying to incorporate them into her overall awareness. This sounds a bit touchy-feely for the average cowboy just trying to sit a horse better, but it really works, I promise.

Runner's Stretch/Legless Horseman

Runner's stretch (which we practiced at the standstill) and legless horseman are actually two parts of the same exercise. The legless horseman is a more advanced version of runner's stretch, which tests balance and connection to the saddle.

Keep the horse walking as part of the challenge of runner's stretch at the walk. Ask the rider to put the outside hand on the horn or pommel for balance. Just as she did in the standstill, she gradually bends her inside knee and reaches back with her inside hand to grab her ankle (or as close as she can get) to gently pull the foot toward the buttocks. Riders with tight quads will have trouble here—have them do the best they can. There's a little trick to getting a good stretch: instead of asking the rider to pull the ankle toward the buttocks, ask the rider to feel her knee pushing toward the ground. This

Runner's stretch at the walk lengthens the thighs and lightens the lower leg.

gives the rider a deeper stretch through the quads and opens the hip flexors. Make sure the rider stays completely upright in her upper body—no leaning or tilting once she's grabbed her lower leg. If she can't reach her ankle without overarching her back, ask her to grab her shin instead, or try an even easier version by just bending the knee and pushing the thigh back.

Limber riders who manage the runner's stretch without much problem can move on to legless horseman, which is the same exercise, but with both legs. The rider memorizes the feeling that the lower leg is soft and weightless while inactive, yet the upper leg is balanced and hanging straight down. The rider is sitting tall and straight, and her "pole"—the imaginary stick that runs down her spine—is through the center of the horse to the ground.

To achieve the legless horseman, most riders will have to lean forward. With the inside arm and leg first, the rider reaches down to grab the ankle and brings it slowly back toward her thigh. Without releasing the inside leg, she reaches for the outside leg with her outside hand. Unless the rider really wants to maintain the position for longer, one circuit is enough for this rather dynamic stretch. Legless horseman works the correct muscles only if the rider remains in the upright position with the upper body and the hips. The rider should feel a strong connection between her seat and the horse. If the rider leans forward to grab her ankles but doesn't return to the proper upright position, she'll be leaning forward on her crotch. The same is true for the rider who leans backward away from the vertical line. In that case she'll be on the cushioned part of her buttocks. Contact between the seat bones and the horse is easier to feel on a closer-contact English saddle than a Western saddle, but either way, in this position the rider can feel a strong connection to the horse through her seat.

The legless horseman position is one of those exercises in this book that demands attention from both longeur and rider because of its relationship to balance in the upper body. Legless horseman builds the feeling of torso stability at the walk. The exercise helps the rider open the upper leg and hip joints, and develop mobility in these crucial muscles. It also places the thigh into the correct position for most equestrian disciplines, with the exception of jumper riders who prefer a short stirrup and more forward leg angle overall. However, even those who ride in a forward seat can benefit from loosening the hips and legs.

Frog Legs

Although the sequences in these chapters don't have to be followed in this order, some exercises naturally go together. I like to follow legless horseman with frog legs, because it's the opposite stretch. Frog legs is a particular favorite of children, probably because it feels a bit funny and has an amusing name. Contrary to legless horseman, it may be necessary for the rider to lean back off her center to get into frog leg position. The longeur should remind the rider not to slump, even as she's bringing her legs up to her chest.

The opposite of runner's stretch is frog legs. Here the rider has both legs up and is balanced on her seat bones. Her upper body remains straight.

With one hand on the pommel or horn and the other on the cantle, the rider lifts both legs and bends both knees, bringing them as close as possible to her chest. Flexible riders will be able to do this with some ease, but the trick is balancing on the seat bones while the horse is walking. Your rider will need to tuck her pelvis slightly. She may feel as if she's rocking side to side. Have the rider maintain the position for four or five strides holding onto the saddle. If she's fairly comfortable and confident in this position, she can let go of her handholds. If she still wants more challenge she can put her arms out to the sides and ride a circle or two.

Frog on a Bike

Frog on a bike is simple and is performed just as it sounds. The rider, in the frog position, can begin by moving just the inside leg and keeping the outside leg in the frog position. The rider gently relaxes the leg and brings it up, as if pedaling that too-small bike from the previous chapter. Once she's moved one leg, the longeur will ask her to move the other leg, with one leg up while the other is down, just like pedaling.

This motion is good practice for learning to sit a horse with a bouncy trot. A gentle pedaling feeling in the legs in time with the horse's hind leg motion can stabilize a rider who's being jolted at the trot. Here we exaggerate the motion quite a bit. The longeur asks the rider to time her leg motions to the horse's walk (inside, outside, inside, outside). To put some muscle burn into the motion, the longeur can ask the rider to slow down the pedaling to four counts per leg (inside, two-three-four, outside, two-three-four). Lifting the leg while holding the body upright involves engaging the lower abdominal muscles rather than the leg muscles. It's similar to an unmounted abdominal crunch exercise, in which the exerciser is lying on the ground pedaling her legs in the air. On the ground you intensify the exercise by lifting the upper back. On horseback, the rider keeps her trunk, shoulders, and hips in alignment as much as possible, balancing lightly on the seat bones while also "connecting" to the horse's walk by allowing some movement in the hips.

MORE LEGS AND HIPS

The most graceful riders sit astride a horse as if they are part of the animal's fluid movement. Separating, stretching, and working each of our body parts can help them to move together with more grace. Lower body exercises at the walk free the hips and legs from the tether of our trunks. Loose hips and legs allow enough flexibility for the rider to keep the trunk and upper body stable and silent. That's what I like to call it: a silent upper body.

Fluffy Legs

You may have heard good legs described as wet towels, cuddly legs, or stubby legs (as I noted earlier). Remember that video of the world championship dressage competition, in which I witnessed the leg fluff in action? The rider canters down centerline, halts at X, salutes the judge, and then, in a somewhat unsightly moment, opens both her legs and pulls them out and away from the saddle. Then she canters on to finish her Grand Prix test.

The purpose of such movement is to reset the seat bones and loosen the thighs—a point of tension for many riders, even those riding at the highest levels. The leg fluff, as I call it, is the ultimate positioning tool. Western or English riders can benefit. Practice the leg fluff after the other leg stretches. After you've pedaled the bicycle for a circle or two, your hip flexors should be nicely warmed up and you'll minimize the risk of cramping a hip flexor or pulling a muscle.

To execute the fluff, the rider lifts both legs away from the saddle (she can hold onto the horn, bucking strap, or pommel to intensify the move-ment while keeping herself upright), slides both legs back behind the girth line, and brings them down again gently. Once the rider has the hang of the leg-fluff action, the longeur can count the three motions of the fluff. "Out," "back," and "down" are the three key words. The four beat count would go, "Out, back, down, rest. Out, back, down, rest." Later, you can try the fluff at the sitting trot, with and without stirrups, where it's particularly useful in releasing a gripping upper thigh.

LEG AND TORSO COMBOS

Centering: a key word for the equestrian disciplines. If the horse's spine is aligned with the rider's spine, riding is a lot easier for both parties. Leg and torso combinations really emphasize centering. Twisting, turning, and reach-ing help the rider understand how it feels to be centered on horseback, where she can put her hand on her lower belly and feel grounded rather than tilted, tight, or collapsed.

Toe Touches

Toe touches, like those you see in gym warm-ups, work well on horseback too. The rider starts with her arms out to the side. She reaches across her body and touches her left hand to her right toe, rising back to sitting posi-tion by contracting the stomach muscles, particularly the lower abdomi-nals. Toe touches warm the body and activate the muscles that may have stiffened up while working on the legs. They also re-energize the stomach muscles, crucial for quieting a busy upper torso. For another type of toe touch, the rider leans forward to touch her right hand to her right toe. In between, the rider returns to upright with her arms out to the side.

Toe touches require the rider to reach down and touch her toes with her hand either on the same side or on the opposite side of the horse. It's great for stretching the rider's back and building flexibility.

Tail Touches

Tail touches also work the abdominals. It can be challenging to reach all the way back and touch the horse's tail, especially for tense riders who feel safer hunched forward. Leaning back to touch the dock of the horse's tail with the fingertips also stretches the back and shoulders. Watch that the rider's legs don't kick forward toward the horse's shoulders but remain hanging long and loose in the proper position, heels still aligned with hips. Alternating arms, the rider returns to the sitting position in the middle of each cycle. Perform the exercise in one stride. The sequence is reach, hold, sit upright; reach, hold, sit upright. Less agile riders may need more time to return to upright, so the entire cycle might need two strides to execute. The longeur can slow down the count as necessary.

Ear Touches

The longeur can also ask the rider to touch the horse's ears, or more accurately, reach toward the ears. Right hand touches the tail, the rider sits upright, right hand touches the ears, she sits upright, left hand touches the tail, she sits upright, left hand touches ears, back to upright.

The rider should concentrate more on accuracy than speed in this series. I'd prefer to see the rider using the muscles correctly, moving into a strong position and then slowly leaning forward, rather than slumping to reach for the horse's ears. Speeding this up can be disconcerting for the horse; plus, the rider doesn't get the muscular benefit of the exercise. Think of it as isometric bodywork, with emphasis on muscles rather than movement. The longeur can slow the rider down to remind her about the importance of building a strong core body and, as the rider becomes more adept at moving, she can interplay rhythm with muscle usage and strength. There's an added benefit that enhances rider safety: by practicing leaning forward and then righting herself, the rider learns the muscles to engage if she's about to fall off.

Resting

Although this next series is quite physically demanding, I call it "resting" because the posture looks very much like lying around on the horse's back. It's really dynamic from a muscle-usage standpoint. The rider engages her abdominal muscles and slowly leans all the way back. This phase resembles the "down" segment of the sit up or abdominal crunch. If she can, the rider lets her head lie back, to rest on the horse's rump as he walks. Depending on the cantle of the saddle, the rider may be able to fully relax and feel the horse's hind legs rock her head side to side. A too-high cantle, however, puts an unnecessary strain on the rider's lower back that could lead to injury, so rider and longeur should proceed cautiously. If the rider can get her head all the way down to the horse's rump, let her lie there and relax. She can even close her eyes and let the horse's motion gently massage the muscles of her neck as her head rolls side to side. If she can't make it all the way down, this exercise becomes much more active and engaged. Rather than resting, she'll actually be doing a modified version of a sit up, holding her abdominal muscles to keep her in position leaning back but just above the saddle.

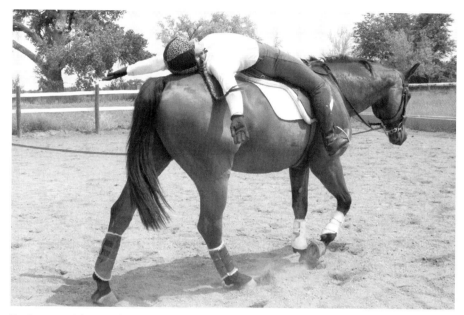

Far from restful, even though the rider here is relaxed, getting into and out of the resting position requires intense abdominal strength.

That sets the stage for the second part of the resting exercise. The longeur directs the rider to come up slowly, and when she's halfway to upright, she holds herself a few inches above the cantle in a half-up, half-down, position, contracting the abdominal muscles to hold herself in place for five to ten seconds. She can continue using her stomach to bring herself back into normal riding position. Only perform this exercise once. It's for building strength rather than solidifying position, and it can be quite taxing.

Horse Hug

Sometimes we just need to give our horses a hug as a way to release tension in the rider and build a relationship with the horse. It also gives the rider's stomach muscles, which may be a little stressed from holding the body up-

The horse hug releases tension in the back and the stomach.

right, a chance to relax and breathe. Hugging a horse in a Western saddle is more challenging than in an English saddle because the horn gets in the way. A Western rider may only be able to hug the horse marginally with just her arms on his shoulders. If the rider is in an English saddle she can lean forward and let her arms drape around the horse's shoulders and neck and rest there, letting the motion of the horse's walk steps rock her side to side.

In both the resting and horse hug exercises (which can also be combined in a sequence, as you'll see at the end of the chapter), the rider may have a tendency to hold her neck tense instead of letting her head drop and rest on the horse. That's not healthy for the neck, plus it changes the focus of the exercise. These exercises are much more effective if the rider can enjoy the slow, rolling motion of the horse's walk step. The longeur's job is to assure the rider that she's in total control of the horse and nothing bad will happen. It may help (if the rider's neck remains tense) to ask the rider to do some of the four-count breathing exercises discussed in the earlier chapter. Deep breathing exercises bring the focus into the rider's center, away from the tense part of the rider's body.

A word about the legs for both the horse hug and resting exercises: They should remain as much as possible underneath the rider. The tendency will be for the rider to kick her legs out in front of her hips while lying back, and behind her while resting on the horse's neck. Neither position is correct. The legs should hang straight down from the rider's hips.

Some people don't like to put their faces or heads on horses' necks, to which I have no response. Part of the joy of riding is commingling with the horse's odor and getting a little dirty in the process.

WITH STIRRUPS

If you've been practicing the previous exercises without stirrups, note that when the rider picks up her stirrups after an extended period riding without them, they'll feel short. Before adjusting them, however, have the rider complete at least one or two circles to become accustomed to the stirrups again. If they still feel too short the longeur might check to be sure the stirrups are the correct length for the rider's particular discipline. Regularly working on the longe line without stirrups lengthens and strengthens the leg. Over time, riders with a regular longe practice might find they have to lower their stirrups because their legs have gotten stronger and longer.

Working with the stirrups, you can begin exercises that engage the strength of the legs to balance. Many beginning riders, when learning to post to the trot, put all their weight in that sliver of foot that's resting on the stirrup bar, instead of using the calf and abdominal muscles to lift themselves out of the saddle. The result is an unbalanced rider who tends to fall back or forward with each up-down of the post. That same rider may also depend on the reins and hands for balance, disrupting the gentle, steady contact to the bit.

To start, the rider moves with the horse, her hips following the swinging motion of the horse's hips. The longeur directs the rider to let her leg hang loosely against the horse's side with an open and flexible hip. The heel hangs aligned with the hip and the shoulder. The sequences of exercises with the stirrups involve the whole leg, not just the foot.

Posting at the Walk

First, ask the rider to stand in her stirrups. The rider can grab the mane, the pommel, or the horn. If the rider is standing on the ball of her foot, with a braced ankle and curled toes, her leg won't move at all. Her inner thigh and calf muscles will be flexed instead of softly relaxed. But in the correct position, she's sinking into her heel and allowing her calf muscle to significantly lengthen downward and stretch, her leg will move back just a bit.

Have the rider remain standing up for at least a half a circle. Then ask her to gently lower herself back to the saddle, using her stomach muscles for support. Contracting the abdominals will keep the rider from falling backward and landing hard on the horse's back.

Perform the exercise in a sequence of sit-five, stand-five. As the rider becomes sure of herself and can stand and sit gently, the longeur might ask the rider to gradually loosen her grip on the saddle or mane. If she becomes unsteady she can always hold on again. Eventually she'll be able to stand in the stirrups for an entire circle without holding on. After some practice the rider will bring herself to standing without the help of the mane or horn.

A more challenging version of posting at the walk involves moving the arms in the same patterns we used earlier in this chapter. Have the rider try to balance in the standing position with her arms pointing to the sky and her hands and fingers flexed, palms turned inward. This position requires centering over the rider's long and stretched legs. A positional fault will become instantly noticeable: if her legs are too far in front of the vertical line or too far behind it, the rider falls backward or forward. The next step is to have the rider put her arms out to the sides for a few strides, then back over her head, then toward the horse's ears. All these will test the rider's balance, particularly during the transitions between arm positions.

The posting-at-the-walk exercise can be modified to a "double up," also very useful for testing a rider's leg position. The rider stands, allowing her leg to move gently back about two inches at most. Once the leg is in position, the longeur asks the rider to slowly and gently resume a seated position *without moving or changing her leg position.* This is a lot harder than it sounds, especially for riders who spend more time behind a desk in front of a computer than on horseback. Tight hip flexors drag the leg out of position. The longeur should ask the rider to stand again, reposition, and try to sit again. Count two strides in the up position and one stride in the down position. The exercise has several benefits, one of which is controlling a body part with directed mental energy rather than just allowing it to fall naturally back to its original position. This develops an independent leg that moves separately from the torso and hip flexor as much as anatomically possible.

Now is a good time for a body check. The rider should tell you without looking where her lower leg is in relation to the point of her hip. Every rider is different—some substantially so—but the basic position of the lower leg should be the same whether the rider is tall, short, large, or small. Once the rider sits back down (always gently), remind her to stack her neck vertebrae one on top of the other—no jutting chins or "duck neck." Ask the rider to slide her chin and jaw back and forth as if she's opening and closing a drawer. The sliding action helps the find the center point where her head is balanced directly over her neck. The rider can also slide the chin and jaw back and forth while looking left and right, respectively. This nice stretch is also a good way to square the head and shoulders. The head weighs ten pounds, more or less, and is the single heaviest part of the body, so its position influences both horse and human. It's easy to let the head drop and the shoulders slouch.

Transitions within the Gait

An aid from the rider can be so subtle the longeur won't see it. But if the aid was correct, the horse will react. Ultimately, the longeur has only her eye to determine what has caused the horse to change his demeanor. During transitions within the gait, we're developing the most quiet signals from the rider to control the horse. Up until now, the longeur has been asking the horse to walk and whoa. Now we give control to the rider.

The longeur asks the horse to step off at the walk very strongly—as forward a walk as your horse partner can manage without breaking into a trot or a jig. As the horse walks forward, the longeur becomes passive, with the whip in the neutral position under her arm, merely directing the horse on the circle. The rider, in the meantime, uses only her seat to slow the rhythm of the walk. If her hips are following and soft, all the rider needs to do is resist the motion of the walk with her lower abdominals. Although she'll have the urge to squeeze her buttocks, that sends tension from the rider's seat to the horse. A gentle slowing of the motion, merely by sinking deeper into the saddle through the pelvis while simultaneously growing taller in the spine, serves to still the proper muscles, sending the right signal to the horse.

Although the motion is described in multiple steps, it actually takes place all at once. There's a slight period of warning for the horse—a momentary squeeze of the inner thighs to signal that he needs to pay attention to the rider, and then the deepening of the seat and lengthening of the spine at once. It may take practice for the horse to hear you. Some horses are more sensitive than others, so the longeur might have to help with a gentle tug on the longe line the moment the rider asks for the change in pace. In some cases, the horse on the longe becomes so attuned to the longeur rather than the rider that it might take a little longer for the horse to understand that the rider is now in control. Once he's responded to the rider, the longeur and rider both relax and praise the horse.

Next the rider releases her abdominals and gives the horse a gentle squeeze with her lower leg, following more actively with her seat. We want to see a real difference within the gait, from a forward free-moving walk to a more "collected" walk with shorter steps. To keep the horse moving forward, complete a whole circle of forward walk, a few strides of shortened walk, then forward again. Once the horse and rider get the idea, the longeur remains passive, allowing the rider to determine what she needs to do with her seat and how quickly she needs to do it.

Walk-Halt Transitions

The same exercise works with walk-halt transitions, with similar aids and preparations. The difference is that that rider holds the motion while at the same time exhaling, to signal the horse to walk into the halt. The first time she tries it, the rider might need to take a little feel of the reins if they're available, to signal that she wants the horse to stop.

A more advanced version shortens the time between the transitions. Once the horse understands what's being asked of him and can differentiate between the rider's "walk slowly" and "halt" aids, you can do a series, such as walk-halt, walk-forward, walk-short, walk-forward, halt. Such rapid-fire transitions sharpen the horse to the aids—he'll be listening more intently to the rider and will react much faster. It also tunes the rider's aids to the horse.

Sometimes a rider squeezes too hard, becomes too tense, or kicks instead of urges the horse forward. Eventually she'll learn just how much leg she needs to use to ask the horse to go forward and how intensely she needs to hold her body to collect the horse's walk. The degree and timing will vary from horse to horse, but such subtlety and communication are the goals of longeing. Start with a whisper of an aid, and if the horse responds well, whisper more quietly. If he doesn't respond, he's probably saying, "Hey, I don't understand," or "I don't hear you." Sometimes he'll respond as if "You're talking too loudly" and he trots instead of walking. The more responsive the horse becomes—and if you practice this exercise a lot it will make him very attuned to the rider—the quicker the transitions can become. For example, with a good communication channel between the horse and the rider, you can ask for two strides of walk, halt, hold for a count of three, walk for two strides, then a bigger walk for three or four strides, and a halt from that bigger walk until the transitions are clear yet smooth.

The Soft Palate

The last exercise of our walk work won't be visible from the ground, but it will help the rider to become softer and quieter, as well as diffuse tension. Some people have difficulty standing on one leg for the balancing exercises required in yoga. The teacher in one particular class of wobbly students instructed them to focus on a point on the floor while sliding their tongues back along the roof of their mouths. There, they found a slight ridge, and then a transition to a spongier part of the mouth. That's the soft palate.

You can do the same as you're longeing. The longeur can ask the rider to place one hand on the lower back and one hand on the lower stomach, with her thumb resting on the lip of her navel. If the rider is tense or uncomfortable, ask her to concentrate on breathing into her hand. Then ask her to rest her tongue on her soft palate. The rider should be in a state of relaxation and correct equitation, a perfect position from which to start the work at the trot.

Generally I encourage riders and longeurs to focus on one part of the body before moving on to the next. Later, when you've practiced all the arm exercises, leg exercises, and overall body motions, you can combine them.

Series A
  Frog legs
  Frog on a bike
  Leg fluff

Series B
  Arm circles
  Hands clasped behind
  Hands clasped in front

Series C
  Touch tail
  Touch toes
  Helicopters (arms out to
    the side, torso turning)

Series D
  Resting
  Horse hug
  Repeat, using abdominal
    muscles to move through
    the series

Chapter 4
TROT

The trot can be the least comfortable of the horse's four gaits. It can feel like trying to stay on a pogo stick as it hops down the trail or around the arena. That's one reason the nose-dragging, barely trotting gait of the Western pleasure horse was developed; riders have to be able to trot for a long time out on the trail or working cattle, and the Western pleasure horse can accommodate them by keeping the trot smooth and soft. The same is true for the recent popularity of gaited horses, like the Tennessee Walking Horse or the Rocky Mountain Horse. These breeds have become popular trail horses, particularly with older people, for their smooth gaits.

For the majority of horse people, however, the horse's trot is neither smooth nor a pleasure. Beginner riders are more likely to bounce out of the tack at the trot than at the walk or the canter. Dressage riders work for years to develop a solid sitting trot that connects them to the horse. And we all learn how to post so we can stay at the trot for longer periods of time.

Working on the longe line will improve a rider's balance and rhythm at the trot. The rider will learn to ride the trot without using the reins for balance. Longeing helps the rider learn to jump, make smooth trot-walk transitions, and even do leg yields or sidepasses. A rider's particular deficiencies at the trot can be addressed and greatly improved on the longe. Also, the rider can practice staying with the horse during any and all variations in the trot—from a slow, poke-along Western jog to the extended trot of advanced dressage, and everything in between. The best riders (many of whom have spent hours on the longe line) become part of the horse—they follow the horse's motion, moving in harmony rather than bouncing around on the poor animal's back. As Susanne von Dietze's book *Balance in Motion* explains, riders with secure seats have "eliminated the space between themselves and the horse."

Working on the longe at the trot builds positional stability. Nothing really changes about your position as your horse speeds up or slows down. Your leg stays firm and your seat balanced. You learn to regulate the speed of the trot and ride transitions smoothly just with your seat through working on the longe line. A horse that canters and then breaks to trot is often unbalanced for the first few strides. That's a hard trot to ride. The rider bounces, falling behind the motion—a problem that working on the longe can solve. Trot work on the longe can help the rider learn to use her arsenal of aids one by one before she has to put them together on horseback. The longe work helps the rider learn to communicate better with her horse. Indeed, the most secure seat at the trot is developed with practice, and is incredibly important for managing any kind of situation in which a rider finds herself.

While beginners can and should learn to ride the trot on the longe, we're beyond that point here—I'm assuming that the rider can post and sit the trot already.

BASICS

For work at the trot, the longeur needs to be vigilant. It's easy for less balanced and confident riders to become unseated when working on these exercises. The longeur has to be in control of the horse at all times, making sure she can regulate the horse's speed with just her voice. A gentle "easy" or a "whoa" should bring the horse to a slower rhythm; a sharp tug on the longe line should bring the horse back immediately to a walk, which might be necessary if the rider loses her equilibrium. A cluck or voice command should be all it takes to get the horse going enthusiastically; if he doesn't respond, a little wave with the whip should do it.

That brings us to the question of pace: How fast or slow should a horse trot on the longe? The answer depends greatly on what you want to accomplish. If it's a basic question of maintaining a posting rhythm, a solid, forward trot is necessary and helpful because the rider will have a hard time keeping the *up-down* of the posting trot if the horse is barely maintaining the one-two rhythm himself. When the horse's momentum helps the rider feel when she should rise, we'll call it our working trot.

Other exercises might require a slightly slower trot, which makes it easier for the rider to stay in half seat, for example, or to keep her eyes closed comfortably, or to let go of the saddle and put her hand on the horse's tail. Even so, the trot should stay rhythmic. The horse shouldn't be allowed to trot in such a way that the rider doesn't feel clear beats.

There are also times when the rider might need to learn to feel comfortable riding a stronger trot, or even want to practice an extended trot, in which each trot stride is longer and the rider feels more "air time" during the "up" phase of the post. Exercises such as double up, described later in this chapter, work well when the horse's pace is stronger (which doesn't actually mean faster) than normal. It's also appropriate for riders to learn on the longe line to ride the lengthened stride of the trot needed for higher levels of dressage.

Imagine you're out on the trail and you pick up a nice trot. Everything's going fine, but a plastic bag blowing across the trail behind him excites your horse—he spooks forward because his flight instinct has kicked in. Having the ability to simply "calm" your post and bring the horse back down to a slow rhythm can mean the difference between a fun ride and a scary one. Riders should learn to change the pace of the trot by using only their seat and legs. The rider can signal the horse to build a bigger trot just by posting "larger" and adding a little bit of leg or slow the trot by holding her abdominal muscles for briefly longer than normal on the downbeat. Learning to ride the trot without reins, and without falling in front of or behind the motion, is an indispensable skill.

That's why this section contains a lot of exercises that slow and speed the trot within the gait. Even if you never plan to execute a dressage test or need to increase your horse's rhythm to get to the base of a fence, fine tuning your own and your horse's reactions at the trot is a sure path to more equestrian confidence. In addition, it makes the horse more responsive and hones the rider's reflexes.

FIRST STEPS

The tools you'll need for the trot are a bucking strap or a saddle with a horn; a few trotting poles (placed off to the side and well out of the way of your circle for now); and a short jumping crop (you'll find out why later). All these items can be put aside for now. We'll work on basics to start with, and later we'll move into using the poles and crop (no horses were injured in the writing of this book, I promise).

From the walk, the longeur asks the horse to trot gently with a voice command. The rider starts out posting the first few circles to get a feel for the horse's trot. If the rider is unfamiliar with the horse or is just feeling insecure, it's okay to have her hold onto the horn or the pommel until she feels confident enough to let go. Releasing the handhold can be achieved very gently by asking the rider to loosen her grip with one hand, then the other, and then both. Or the rider can keep her hands resting gently on the saddle or on the horse's withers (as long as she doesn't have to lean forward to reach them). The idea is to ground the rider. Imagine flight attendants on a turbulent trip who walk down the aisle of a bouncy airplane by sliding their hands along the baggage compartments to keep themselves grounded. The light touch on the withers is the same idea. The minute the rider feels at all uncertain, have her bring her hands back down to the horse and grab a tuft of mane or the bucking strap, or simply rest a hand on the withers. She'll immediately feel more secure.

Slow Stretch

Once the rider has circled twice around at the posting trot so she feels comfortable, the longeur asks the rider to raise her inside arm straight up so her fingers point to the sky. At the same time she will step deeper into her inside stirrup both during the up and down phase of the post. Here we're stretching out the side of the body, working to overcome the tendency to collapse the rib cage toward the inside of the circle or slump forward on the downbeat of the trot.

Repeat using the outside arm. If the rider is feeling confident and completes two trot circles with each arm stretched up one at a time, ask her to bring both arms over her head quite high and strong. She should be concentrating on opening the area between her hips and the bottom of her rib cage on each side. The upper arms should be parallel to her ears, which requires strong, tight arms and shoulder blades pressing back. The exercise stretches the side of the body and opens the sternum.

During this exercise, the rider might find herself falling backward during the downbeat of the post. If so, have her bring one arm back down, rest it on the bucking strap or horn, and try again until she feels confident she can maintain her posting rhythm and straightness with one arm raised. Then have her gradually loosen her grip with the hand that's holding on, as described earlier, until she's got both arms stretched in the air. She may only be able to ride this way for a few steps before losing her balance again. Regroup and try again, asking the rider to stay in position with both arms overhead for a little longer each time.

Repeating some of the exercises from the walk at the trot adds a layer of challenge. Here the rider is stretching one arm up while posting the trot.

A rider who is constantly falling backwards or forwards has a problem with her posting position. Several issues may be at work here: The rider may be using her upper body rather than her lower legs to post. Or, she may be moving her upper body forward, causing her to ride up the horse's neck while her legs act as a pendulum. Ask her to post by pushing her hips toward the horse's ears. Another way to correct posting trot balance issues is to have the rider hold the rhythm of her post in the downward motion with her abdominal muscles. If neither exercise fixes the problem, focus on the posting trot leg position. The rider might have a weak leg that doesn't support her. Alternatively, she could be gripping with and pivoting from her knees. You might have to move on to leg exercises and return to arms later once the rider has a stronger base of support.

Windmills

Now the longeur can ask for arm windmills, in which the rider rotates both arms around and around in rhythm at the posting trot. The trot pace should be fairly slow so the rider can feel the balance as she moves her arms around. As in the above exercise, she raises her inside arm overhead while stepping deeper into her inside stirrup. Instead of maintaining the arm in the air for several strides, the rider switches arms every count of two. The leg action replicates the "bicycle" motion, stepping down lightly into each stirrup as the arm on the same side rises up. The legs follow the arms. As each arm raises the leg on the same side deepens. The leg movement should be a subtle action—barely perceptible from the ground.

Windmills stretch the arms, the shoulders, the upper back, and the stomach muscles. Here Penny is practicing windmills without stirrups.

Keep the horse moving. The horse may want to slow down or stop abruptly if he feels the rider become unbalanced. It's a natural reaction to a change in rider balance. However, unless the rider is in trouble, the longeur must keep the horse active with a little whip encouragement if necessary. It's good practice for the rider to learn to right herself on horseback and keep going. The only time to stop the horse is when the rider is becoming unseated or risks falling off. Otherwise, keep up the steady trot rhythm.

After a few strides of alternating upward arms, the rider rotates each arm in a big forward circle, in a windmill action as if her hands were bicycle pedals. The longeur reminds the rider to remain tall and stretching. She can also observe whether the rider is fully extending her arms. No weak elbows or half efforts accepted. The rider should work on stretching the shoulder rotator cuffs (which can correct the slumping rider) and on her coordination at the same time. Consider each arm circle as the face of a clock. The rider can move each arm a quarter of an hour with each action of the post. After a few arm circles forward, reverse the arms so they are circling backward.

A more advanced version involves moving the arms in opposite directions at the same time. Practicing oppositional movements such as this is necessary to becoming an effective rider—the ability to move the right arm one way and the left in the opposite direction is fundamental to separating all the parts of the body from each other. Imagine the marionette I described earlier, with each of its segments separated by a joint and attached to a string. That's what we're working toward with many of these exercises.

REFINING THE POSTING TROT

Posting the trot is so fundamental that a lot of us do it without really thinking about whether we're rising and sitting correctly. We just post. Still, a rider can always improve. The exercises below serve to magnify problems with the posting trot position so the rider has an idea of how to improve when she's riding alone. The longeur helps the process by taking a look at the rider as she posts—and asking herself a few questions about the rider's position. It is a learning experience for both rider and longeur, who then can develop a vocabulary for the rider to use later on.

Here are a few common problems and their potential fixes:

- Is the post very high above the saddle?
  The longeur should ask the rider to post with her hips moving toward her hands held in rein position, rather than in an up-down motion. (Note that up-down is what we learned as beginners, but those two words don't quite describe the correct rising trot—it's more of a "forward and down" motion.)

- Is the rider awkward coming down to a seated position?
  Ask the rider to press out and down with the area between her navel and pubic bone to stabilize her lower core (her "center") on the downbeat.

- Does the rider post too far forward and backward, landing toward the back of the saddle instead of the middle, or posting over the pommel?
  The opposite problem of the first point, the longeur will ask the rider to post more vertically.

- Does she lean forward with her upper body in the up beat?
  Remind her to keep her hips and shoulders aligned.

- Is the posting rhythm unclear?
  The longeur can count the "one-two, one-two" beat of the post, and the rider can use a handhold to find the rhythm.

- Is there too much arch in her back, causing her to ride with her butt out behind her?
  Tell her to scoop her pelvis under and forward.

The exercises that follow are meant to repair posting trot problems. Practicing the double up, for example, automatically slides the rider's leg into the correct position so she can post in balance. Practicing double downs helps the rider develop the slight hip swing necessary for sitting the one beat needed to change diagonals. Double downs develop strength in the core to support the upper body in sitting trot. Working with the arms aligns the body and helps the rider become less dependent on the reins for balance.

Double Up

A leg that moves too much, swinging back and forth with each post, destabilizes the upper body. That can be easily solved with what I like to call the "double up" at the posting trot. The rider stands in her stirrups for two beats in the post. Her body is straight up, rather than slightly bent as it is in the half seat. To help the rider verbally, the longeur says, "Down-up-up, down-up-up, down-up-up," and so forth. The double-up exercise underscores positional faults, particularly with the rider's legs. If they are either too loose or gripping too much, the rider will fall backward and her legs will kick out in front of her when she tries to stay up for two counts. If her position is solid with her legs long and hips loose, open, and aligned under her shoulders, she'll be able to stay in the "up" position for the two beats and gently come back to the "down" position in rhythm, immediately rising again to double up.

The longeur can watch how the rider's leg moves when she is in the "up" position. The rider can correct the post position by allowing her leg to slide back two or so inches—which it's naturally inclined to do—as she's holding the double-up position. She gently returns to seated, *without changing her leg position.* The legs should now be aligned with the heel under the hip and the shoulder. Now she can try the double up again; with the legs underneath the rider, she should be able to hold the leg position when she descends for the downbeat. The long leg that's created in the standing position is maintained as the rider returns to sitting. Once in position, the leg rests gently on the horse's side.

Here is where the longeur can really safeguard the rider's good leg position. If the rider's leg is stretched long, she can maintain a cuddling feel with her lower legs. Her calves, held in this position, help her to rise with her leg correctly under her. She should be able to gently sit down, without the leg swinging up and forward and without pinching. It's not easy. Staying up requires the rider's concentration and sometimes a handhold on the mane.

To further refine the rising trot, extend the double up so the rider stands in her stirrups for seven or eight strides, or roughly half the circle. The rider will need to keep her balance in precisely the way she did during the double up, without falling forward or backward. Her legs will stretch long and her heels will come softly down, but only if she relaxes her toes and allows her ankles to soften. If she's unable to hold that position for half a circle, see what might be amiss with her leg position, balance, or seat. Her upper body may not be directly aligned with her hips and heels. She may be gripping with her knees or thrusting her body forward. The longeur then asks rider to return to the regular posting trot again for a few strides to reorganize and rest. If the rider still can't hold the "up" position for more than a couple of strides, she simply may not be strong enough, or her position may need more work.

Try this: have the rider put her inside hand on the pommel and the outside hand on the cantle. Sit the trot for a few strides holding on in this way. Ask the rider to do a leg fluff, in which she opens her legs from the hips and slides them back and down underneath her. While continuing to hold onto the saddle, she returns to double up. By holding on, she can try again to maintain the "up" position, using her handholds to steady herself while she slides her legs underneath her hips and shoulders.

Variations on Double Up

On the other hand, a rider who can hold the up position without slipping forward or back and without holding on is ready to move on to an advanced exercise. The rider returns to the regular post for a few strides, then holds the "up" position with her hands stretching tall over her head. After two strides of up, she returns to the posting trot for two beats. Next, she stands in "up" position with her arms out to the side for two beats, returning again to a regular post afterwards. In the third part, she stays in "up" with her arms in front, hands pointing toward the horse's ears. If she can do all of these arm positions separately without losing her balance in the "up" position, you can combine all three: front, up, side. Such movement gives the rider confidence and shows her how little riding has to do with the hands and the reins.

Double Down

After a few rounds of double ups, the rider can practice double downs. The same concept as the double up, she posts the normal rhythm but adds a second "down" beat. The sequence is: *up, down-down; up, down-down*. It's also a good way to practice changing the posting diagonal. The rider should allow her hips to swing just a little bit forward with the double down. Next, the rider can practice two of each: *Up-up; down-down*. You can vary the exercise in several ways. Add three *ups* for every *down* or three *downs* for each *up*. The exercise can even be extended to encompass a half circle of *up* and a half circle of *down*.

Practicing the Half Seat

Another exercise that focuses on balance and is useful for those who would like to jump is the half-seat, full-seat exercise. Even if you have no jumper-ring ambitions, the ability to remain balanced in the half seat will help when you're heading uphill on the trail or trotting over cavalletti, for example. Even dressage and Western riders, who ride with longer stirrups, can benefit from practicing half seat.

I like to start the half-seat, full-seat exercise at the walk, practicing the transition between the two positions a couple of times. Once each position is secure and correct, the exercise can be repeated at the trot. Half seat, which is also called "two-point" because just the rider's two legs are in contact with

Although the rider in the top photo is in a jumping saddle, the half seat is useful for Western and dressage riders as well.

the horse, is just a double up with the rider's knees bent and her body slightly forward at the waist. The pelvis remains tucked, keeping the back flat.

One common fault to watch for is the rider leaning up the horse's neck. The longeur is responsible for making sure the rider's pelvis remains over the very center of the saddle. Riders in a Western saddle won't have this problem, of course—the saddle horn risks poking a hole in your stomach. But this is a very common fault for English riders. Photographs of the finest hunter/jumper riders show their legs remaining under them. Their backs follow the arc of their horse. Their seats remain over the middle of the saddle except in extreme cases when the pair is jumping a particularly large fence. The rider's upper body stays with the horse's motion, the correct position for half seat.

To teach a rider the half-seat position, have her stand straight up in the stirrups; then let all her body weight sink deeply into her heels with a gentle break at the ankles. This may feel awkward at first. Tight calf and hamstring muscles will resist this stretch. The longeur should make sure the rider isn't standing on or curling her toes. The rider uses her calf muscles to hold herself gently above the saddle, with her knees bent. The longeur may even ask the rider to grab the horn, pommel, or bucking strap for security, but a better option is to hold a pinch of mane a third to halfway up the neck. A balanced rider can rest her hands gently on the neck without having to hold on. Once her heels are sunk as low as possible, ask the rider to bend her upper body from the waist to about 45 degrees from upright. If the body represents the hands of a clock and the upright position is six o'clock, the half seat is ten after six.

The rider should hold the half seat for a full circle, after which she can gently (and I emphasize *gently*—think of the horse!) settle back into the center of the saddle. Then the rider can practice holding the half seat for a full circle, followed by sitting trot for two strides, then the half seat for another half circle. Once the rider can gently move between the two positions with ease and without slamming down on her horse's back, speed up the transitions between the half seat and the full seat. The longeur can help by counting the number of strides. Keep it an even number, such as four strides up and four strides down, gradually increasing to two strides up and two strides down.

Drop and Find

It's happened to all of us. You'll be riding along, and one of your feet comes out of the stirrup. And sometimes you need that stirrup *now*. The jump is approaching. The hounds found a scent. You're in the middle of a dressage test. Your trail buddies just took off loping. Whatever the situation, it's nice to know you've practiced finding them at the trot or the canter, so it's really no big deal.

To practice dropping and finding the stirrups at the trot is simple. The rider drops her stirrups at the walk first. Then the longeur asks the horse for a trot, while the rider lets her legs just hang, exaggerating the swinging hips so she stays with the rhythm. The rider can hold onto the bucking strap, horn, or cantle if it's more comfortable. After a few strides, the longeur directs the rider to point the toes on her left foot up and in toward the horse's side to fish around for the stirrup. The rider may need to glance down briefly, but only as a last resort. Looking down unbalances the body, which could be a problem in a less controlled environment. The rider may also need to lift her leg a bit, depending on the type of saddle she's using and the stirrup length. A Western rider may not have to fish around very much at all, while an English rider in a jumping saddle may have to bring her knees and toes up dramatically to find her stirrups.

Once she's found both stirrups, the rider can drop them again (holding on, especially if the horse has a bouncy trot) then gently lift her toes to find the stirrups again, drop them, and then find them. In some instances the action of dropping and finding her stirrups distracts the rider from the fact that she is trotting without stirrups.

That is to say, an unconfident rider sometimes thinks too much—especially during a lesson, when she tries hard to be perfect. That level of concentration actually can make a rider tense. Fearful riders, too, need to know that dropping and finding stirrups while in motion is altogether possible. The activity moves the rider's focus from her posture or fear to action—which is what happens when you're riding and not focusing on position. So her legs and body get a little floppy and loose—not a bad thing, overall, because flexibility and adjustability are very important to effective riding and an independent seat.

After the rider has dropped and picked up the stirrups successfully, return to the walk and readjust the rider's seat. It's important to do so periodically after a series of trot circles. It gives the horse and rider time to breathe and a minute to relax, and allows the longeur to pinpoint positional faults or areas of tension.

Sitting Trot

Dropping and finding the stirrups is a great way to introduce the sitting trot work. Fundamental to becoming a balanced rider is being able to sit the trot with connection, without gripping through the knees or holding onto the saddle, or—worse yet—"water skiing" by leaning on the reins to keep balance. The goal is to remain balanced no matter what the horse is doing.

The sitting work should begin with the horse trotting in a strong rhythm. The longeur may be tempted to slow the trot to keep the rider comfortable, but don't do so unless the horse has a very bouncy gait and the rider is really unable to sit comfortably while holding on. Slowing the horse down to a toe-dragging trot doesn't help the rider develop balance; it only creates the habit of allowing the horse to trot slowly, and the rider doesn't have the opportunity to learn to sit the working trot correctly. Better to start out at the beginning with a correct, rhythmic pace rather than taking the easy way out.

Have the rider (with stirrups) relax into the saddle, placing one hand on the horn or bucking strap. Whatever method she's using to hold on, the rider should remain tall. As in the other exercises we've done, check the rider's position right away. Are her legs underneath her? Are her heels down and eyes up and forward, following the circle through the horse's ears? Are her hips moving dynamically with the horse's hips?

Head Rolls

Ask the rider to bend her head forward, touching her chin gently to her sternum. Then ask her to lift her head to normal position. Note that moving the head while trotting increases the rider's mobility and adjustability; if the rider has thrust her chin forward and bounces her head, bending the neck can correct it. Another common fault is the rider that tilts her head to the inside of the circle, collapsing her corresponding shoulder and ribcage. Working on head and neck mobility can correct that problem, too.

Now ask the rider to turn her head from side to side and forward and backward in rhythm with the sitting trot (it's okay for the rider to be holding on). Use the rhythm of the trot: one stride with head down, one with head up and back, one stride with head turned right and one stride with head turned left.

Eyes Closed

Next, ask her to close her eyes as the horse trots around the longeing circle. If she's not seasick, continue. If she is, have her open her eyes to avoid getting nauseous, and ask her to focus on the "third eye"—the soft focal point that's above the bridge of the nose between the eyebrows, which we practiced at the walk. The idea here is to release the tension in the eyes that develops when a rider is concentrating. Another relaxation exercise for a rider who can't close her eyes during the sitting trot is to open her mouth wide, sliding her jaw back and forth, making a kind of "argh" sound. It may look ridiculous, but a lot of the tension in the mouth, neck, and head travels down the body, tightening the seat and causing the rider to bounce rather than connect with her seat bones to the horse's trot.

Trotting around with your eyes closed can teach the rider so much about riding. It allows her to feel the horse, as well as to relax and breathe into the trot. As I noted earlier, some of the exercises in this book are meant to take the rider's attention to a different place. To be effective, the rider needs to be both thinking *and* feeling. As you improve at your chosen discipline, you begin to ride with more feel rather than analysis. But a rider's trust in her senses can be greatly enhanced by closing her eyes and describing what the horse and her body are doing. It tunes her in.

A rider who is comfortable with her eyes closed can concentrate on moving her hips in concert with her horse's hind legs. Help her develop feel by telling her which leg is moving forward. As the left hind leg lifts up, under, and forward, the longeur says "left"; and then the same with the right hind. The longeur can get the rider started, then let her feel it for herself. To the rider, it will feel like her hip is moving up as the horse's leg in motion is coming up and forward. A rider who is very tight in her hips will be unable to tell which leg is moving. If that's the case, you'll need to skip to hip opening exercises. A valuable one for the rider who grips too much involves, with eyes closed, lifting her inside arm over her head, stretching as high as she can. This exercise opens and loosens the area between the hip and ribcage, where much of the rider's tension resides.

As the rider trots around getting a feel for the horse's gait and telling the longeur which leg is coming up and forward, ask her also to tell you what she's feeling:

- How are her hips moving with the horse?

- What parts of her body are resisting the horse's motion?

- Where are there points of tension in her body?

- Which of the horse's legs are moving, including the front ones?

If the rider is really being jolted around and bouncing hard on the horse's back, ask her to post the trot to reorganize (with her eyes *still closed*) before returning to sitting. The eyes stay closed for one or two circles.

Alternate Sitting and Posting

Next up: Sitting and rising in alternation. The rider sits the trot for half the circle, then posts for one or two strides. Switching between the two actions can help the rider develop a firm midsection (better than hours of sit-ups, I promise) and smoothness. The longeur is responsible for correcting the rider if she's pitching forward into the rising trot, instead of posting with her hips forward to her hands (on the bucking strap, or carried in rein position). If all is going well, the rider keeps her eyes closed while counting out the strides, "One-two-three-four" while sitting and "One-two-three-four" while rising. Like the double-up exercise discussed in the last section, this will build a firm sense of rhythm.

One way to develop a quiet sitting trot is to lengthen the amount of time the rider spends sitting, alternating it with periods of rising trot. The sitting-rising sequences each last as long as half a circle. During the half circle of sitting, have the rider raise her arms out the sides, stretching through the side of her body and down through the lower leg and heel to open the shoulders, lift the chest, and lengthen. When she's rising, her hands are in rein position. Alternate between the two positions so she completes a half circle of sitting trot with arms out and a half circle of posting with hands held in rein position.

This exercise builds hand position awareness. The rider concentrates on finding her rein position when she resumes the posting trot, and on balance and steadiness without the reins at the sitting trot.

A Test for the Longeur

Don't forget to change directions frequently. The most balanced horse and rider team tracking right might be the most uncoordinated going left—both horses and people have good and bad sides. See if you (the longeur) can identify the differences in both rider and horse tracking left and right. Point those out to the rider. The longeur can also ask the rider to identify her weak side, or the horse's stiff side, and verbalize how that feels. Once you've identified those differences, you can work on exercises specifically addressing the idea of symmetry (a nearly impossible goal) in riding.

ARMS AT SITTING TROT

Riding well really comes down to being able to do two or three things at the same time while staying attuned to the horse. To arrive at that stage requires breaking down the body into its separate parts, strengthening and coordinating those pieces, and finally putting it all together.

Adding arm movements to exercises at the posting and sitting trot helps a rider become even more coordinated. The goal is to mold the rider to the horse. An effective rider is malleable, flexible, and firm. She's able to move in a controlled but soft manner. Working on the longe line builds the foundation for that position—think of each series as the raw material that's added along the way to build the total rider.

In sitting trot, moving the arms adds a dimension to a rider's ability to balance. To begin, practice the simple arms-overhead exercise we worked on at the standstill, walk, and posting trot. The longeur asks the horse for a steady trot, and the rider raises her arms high

While sitting the trot, the rider can test her balance by changing the position of the torso and arms.

overhead, pointing her fingertips to the sky, while at the same time lengthening down through the thigh and into the lower leg. Her core body should be firm with her hips moving with the horse's steps. The rider can breathe deeply into her core, slightly inflating her stomach and gently tightening the diaphragm to hold her balance.

There is a fine line between a strong yet flexible core and a tight one. The rider who appears more like a stone statue holding her position for all she's worth is just as incorrect as the rider bouncing all over the saddle. The tight rider may be tense in her lower back, or her hips may be out behind her. A tuck of the pelvis, while slightly holding the muscles of the lower stomach, can help the rider sit the trot better. The diaphragm collects and absorbs the bounce. Raising the arms overhead at the sitting trot is good for riders who tend to cramp their legs up and grip with their knees, or slouch with their upper bodies leaning too far forward.

Slow Arms

We worked on windmills at the walk and at the posting trot. This exercise is similar, except that the rider brings her arms together in between sweeping each arm back. It's performed at the sitting trot. First, the right arm swings back to point to the tail, and the left arm swings forward. After two strides, reverse. It is okay in this exercise for the rider's torso to move to the inside and outside, as long as her hips stay aligned with the horse's shoulders. Another way to do it is to bring the left arm back, pointing to the tail. Then bring the left arm even with the right arm, so both point to the ears. Now switch: right arm to tail, left arm to ears. Later exercises will involve more torso action, but for now we're stretching the arms and shoulders out to work on slumping and balance at the sitting trot.

Connecting with Center

Another exercise begins with the rider putting two hands on her helmet, and rubbing circles on her head. Then the longeur asks the rider to slowly move the inside hand to the area just below her navel—her center. She pushes out against her hand with each trot step, "inflating" and then "deflating" the stomach. Then ask her to switch hands, placing her navel hand on her helmet and the opposite hand on her stomach. This is a great exercise to get the rider concentrating on something besides the horse's bouncy trot. It identifies the rider's center of gravity so she can find her balance quickly. It helps her to connect her center gently with the horse.

Shoulder Rolls

To ensure the position of the rider's shoulders and body between exercises, the rider's hips should be loose and swinging, with her hands resting behind her thighs on the horse's upper flanks. A rider who is relaxed and deep in the saddle has her shoulder blades back and down. Rolling alternate shoulders at the sitting trot diffuses accumulated tension in the upper back and shoulders. Post two or three strides to rebalance the body, and then roll the left shoulder, then the right shoulder, so the rider's whole trunk moves slightly side to side, but not off center. Then the rider should roll both her shoulders in the same direction, making sure each shoulder truly goes back behind the vertical to adjust and loosen them.

Torso Stretches

Have the rider put her hands on her waist and turn her torso to the inside, while feeling both seat bones evenly weighted and securely in contact with the saddle. Then have the rider turn to the outside of the circle. Watch that both seat bones stay nicely seated and even, hips and shoulders level. As the rider turns, the seat bone on the opposite side may lighten slightly. But overall as the torso moves left and right, the rider's seat and hips don't change—everything continues to swing softly and lightly with the horse's motion while the rider's hips remain in alignment with her shoulders.

SWINGING TROT TECHNIQUES

The graceful dressage rider, the flawless hunter rider, or the cowboy who seems glued to the saddle got there from hours of practice sitting the trot. It's not an easy gait to sit, as we know. But there are some other techniques to soften the rider's body.

After the rider has placed her hands on her hips, she can place her outside hand in rein position and her inside hand behind her back. Here she can gently feel the swing of the horse's trot and the relationship between the horse's center and her own spine. The rider's back should be flat with only a gentle arch. Too much arch and the rider's butt will be out behind her, causing her to fall forward onto her crotch. Too little arch and the rider's back becomes hard. Stiffness prevents her from feeling the horse's swing and a much bouncier trot will ensue as the horse fights the tightness. If the longeur discovers either of these conditions she directs the rider to describe what parts of her body are working against the horse rather than with him. The rider will hopefully identify how an overarched or overly straight back hinders the horse's movement. Here the longeur may ask the rider to tuck her pelvis, swing her hips more aggressively, or "bicycle" with her legs, stepping down in each stirrup in rhythm with the trot to loosen the hips and soften the seat.

For an overarched back, the rider should scoop her pelvis up and underneath her, so she is sitting on a triangle of seat bones and crotch. Alternatively, she can press her stomach back toward her spine while keeping her upper body from collapsing forward. A third exercise involves the rider posting for a stride or two up and over her legs, pressing her pelvis forward toward her hands, in rein position. As she's posting upwards, ask her to scoop her pelvis underneath her. Then, without changing anything about her position, she can gently return to sitting trot.

With one hand behind her back and one in rein position, the rider can level the shoulders, open the chest, and flatten the back. She can use this position to regulate her four-count breath (discussed in Chapter 1), holding her hand on her stomach as she breathes and switching hands with each series of four. Another technique is to practice changing the pace of the trot by pressing the hand on her stomach down while pressing the hand on her back up. This action aids the rider feel the necessary body position to slow down the trot. She can also use this position to help her to scoop her pelvis at the canter.

Horseback Dance

The rider with the tight back can be helped only with relaxation and strengthening exercises, along with more hours in the saddle. True, some horses have really uncomfortable trots, but sitting to them can be improved with some deep breathing and what I like to call the horseback dance. It involves moving the whole torso, side-to-side, letting the horse's swing travel all the way from the horse's hindquarters into the rider's shoulders. She can wiggle her midsection and swivel her shoulders from side to side. The longeur can ask the rider to step down deeply in her stirrups and move her whole body as she does, shifting the position of her arms and shoulders as much as the horse will tolerate without getting excited. The rider returns to the position of one hand on the reins and one behind the back after she's shaken the kinks out of her body.

Not just the stiff rider will benefit from the horseback dance. It helps the frightened, tense, or fearful rider realize she can move around in the saddle without any internal fears being realized ("I'll fall off," "The horse is going to run off with me," "I'm not in control here"). She'll become more confident. With her hands on her stomach and back, she'll feel centered and grounded on the horse.

For the horseback dance exercise, the rider should let herself go and move however she likes. Just like in dancing, the rider can wiggle on the horse. This is one of the few in my collection of exercises that encourages floppy arms, soft muscles, and plenty of movement in the saddle. Most of the other exercises require concentration on correct positioning. With the horseback dance, there's no right or wrong, just movement of the body.

VARYING THE PACE

The rider and the longeur should work on changing the horse's pace using only the rider's seat and legs. Using changes in "air time" in the *up* part of the post and the tension in her stomach muscles in the *down*, the rider will learn how to time her aids correctly, as well as learn to control the horse with just her seat. Such refinement is key to building an "educated" seat that can communicate quietly to the horse. It's certainly a better alternative to a bouncing, flailing, or pulling rider (we've all been there, don't forget). That only annoys the horse.

Bigger Trot Steps

To practice changing paces with just the post rhythm, the longeur asks the horse to trot more forward than his normal pace on the longe. From here, the longeur asks the rider to follow with a bigger post—adding a fraction of a second of airtime to each "up." Here the rider should be able to feel the horse's bigger step. The rider can squeeze slightly with her legs on each "up" beat. Experiment with how little it takes to ask the horse to go forward. If there is no response, the rider squeezes just a little more firmly while the longeur encourages the horse onward with the whip.

Smaller Trot Steps

Now the rider slows her post. Using just her abdominal muscles, she holds herself slightly longer in the downbeat. The rider is gentle with her request—

the sensitive horse asked to slow his pace too harshly may come crashing back to a walk, landing squarely on his forehand.

The rider can experiment with how much aid she needs for the horse to react. If the horse doesn't "hear" the rider's engagement of the abdominals and slower post, the longeur may have to tug gently on the line to remind the horse to listen to the rider. With practice, the horse will become responsive to both the forward and the slower aids, and the longeur can remain a passive presence. Once the horse is listening to the rider, she can vary the pace by asking for a half circle of big trot strides and a half circle of smaller strides. The horse should take no more than one or two strides to react to the rider. As the horse and rider both react faster, the rider can ask for even quicker transitions, eventually working toward changing the pace each quarter of a circle.

Try it at the sitting trot. The longeur remains passive with her whip under her arm as a signal to the horse that the rider is now in control. The rider asks the horse, with one light touch of the legs, to move forward into a bigger trot, swinging her hips in the sitting trot more actively. The rider can then slow the trot by sinking a little deeper through her lower stomach, closing her upper thighs, holding with her abdominal muscles, and thinking "slower" with her body.

Beware of a few common faults: the rider shouldn't fall forward during the transition to the slower trot. Her position stays directly on the vertical line, parallel to the horse's body, when she asks for the bigger trot. Some riders fall behind the vertical, leaning back to stay with motion or to drive the horse forward. Instead, leaning back drives the rider's seat into the horse's back and impedes the motion. I emphasize that the rider's position doesn't change during the transition.

Walk-Trot Transitions

The transitions from big trot to slow trot prepare the horse to listen to the rider's seat. Use the same aids for the walk-trot transitions. The rider needs to only add a little bit of strength to the downward transition. Again, the longeur may need to remind the horse with a "whoa" command timed to the action of the rider's aid.

The longeur must watch closely that the rider holds her spine straight and tall during the transition and keeps her legs on the horse in a gentle, cuddly squeeze. The action of the rider's legs around the horse's belly help to lift the horse's back, supporting him into a round transition, rather than dropping him into unorganized downward transition where he falls on his forehand. After a few strides in trot and a few strides in walk, the rider can shorten the length of time between the two, so the horse trots three strides, walks two, and so on until the transitions are quick and easy.

WORKING WITHOUT STIRRUPS

Back when I used to teach summer camp riding lessons, I'd make all the campers drop and cross their stirrups. I'd give each student a dollar bill to put under their leg. Then I'd teach an entire forty-five-minute lesson, and the last rider who still had her dollar won all the money. It was a nice incentive for the kids, and a good way to build up leg strength in little, and sometimes lazy, riders.

Indeed, what may seem like cruelty actually built stamina and coordination. Today, when there's no one around to longe me, I work at the trot without stirrups. Although some riding instructors love to torture riders by making them trot for hours on end without stirrups, you should do so only if you are balanced enough to stay on without gripping with your knees, and can post using only your lower leg muscles.

While riding without stirrups builds confidence and helps the rider develop muscles necessary for good equitation, it also occasionally encourages some bad habits. Watch good riders carefully—notice their knees and upper thighs stay open and soft *until needed*, while their seats remain firmly

Crossing the stirrups over the withers keeps them from banging against the horse's sides while you're working on the trot. You can hold onto the bucking strap to keep yourself from bouncing out of the saddle.

connected to the horse and their legs stay long. Less skilled riders working without stirrups will pinch with their knees, causing them to pop up and out of the saddle, thus effectively eliminating any connection they have with the horse's back. Those same riders, fearful of that speedy, unbalanced trot that horses develop with a tense rider on their backs, tend to become tight during transitions.

As an example, a well-trained horse should pick up the canter from the trot with just a touch of aids. Beginner or unbalanced riders tend to squeeze with their knees, and then, as a reaction to being pinched out of the saddle, squeeze their thighs. The horse reacts by trotting faster and faster because the tension on his spine doesn't allow his back to come up and his hind legs to step underneath his body, actions necessary for the canter transition. That's why I caution you to use the stirrup-less exercises carefully and correctly. Otherwise you'll be creating a problem rather than a solution.

Stirrup-Free Posting

Nonetheless, riding without stirrups is fundamental to improving. While some may argue that posting without stirrups creates a tight leg rather than a tight-but-flexible leg, there's no denying that posting without stirrups is one of the best isometric exercises you can do. In riding schools all over the world, students spend a great deal of time on the longe line posting without their stirrups to build leg strength and coordination. As children taking riding lessons, we've probably all trotted without stirrups. Riding instructors know posting without stirrups builds the proper leg muscles (calves, in particular). A beginner who hasn't mastered the posting rhythm needs to wait to try it until she can follow the horse's rhythm while posting with stirrups, then do so at different rhythms such as a longer-strided trot and a more collected trot.

In English tack, begin by dropping both stirrups and pulling the stirrup leather buckle down a couple of inches. Then cross the right stirrup over the horse's withers, and the left stirrup over the right. Crossing the stirrups keeps them from banging against the horse's sides. With the buckles pulled down, the metal won't interfere with the rider's thighs.

A rider who already posts the trot rhythmically can use one hand to help her out of the saddle for the up beat, but over time she should be able to post using calf muscles only. The rider doesn't have to rise far, but she does have to maintain a clear "up-down" rhythm. Begin with just a few strides, alternating with sitting trot for three or four strides and posting for two strides while holding on with one hand. Gradually increase the posting time and loosen your grip, until you are able to post the trot for at least a couple of circles without stirrups and without holding on. The longeur makes sure the rider's arms and hands aren't bouncing up and down with each post. The hands and arms remain placed in front of her in steady rein position. Elbows should open and close with each up and down respectively, but the hands remain quiet.

Leg Fluff at the Trot

A rider who is very comfortable sitting the trot without her stirrups can do almost all the exercises we did at the walk at the sitting trot. The rider sits the trot, letting her legs hang long with her thighs loose, toes up, knees and toes rotated in so the leg lies flat. If the rider begins to look unbalanced or "pop" out of the saddle, tell her to put one hand on the bucking strap or horn, and open both hips by taking the legs away from the saddle two inches. The rider should use her hip and thigh muscles. She slides her legs back a few inches and places them against the saddle. This is an extremely difficult exercise for people who sit at a desk all day—they tend to have tight hips and are frequently unable to do the "leg fluff" without cramping their hip flexors.

Earlier we talked about the rider "popping" out of the saddle when she begins to grip too much with her inner thigh and knee. Leg fluffs remedy this problem. The exercise opens the inner thigh and reinforces the seat's connection with the horse.

Torso Twists

Another interesting exercise while sitting the trot, if your rider is able to let go of the bucking strap without falling forward or bouncing out of the saddle, involves moving the torso side to side, this time while holding the arms straight out. The rider turns to the inside of the circle and then to the outside, again following the rhythm of the trot. It may even be helpful for the

Torso twists at the sitting trot reinforce the centering necessary for the rider to stay with the horse.

longeur to count out loud, "One-two-three-four, turn, one-two-three-four, turn." The rider should keep her thighs open and loose, her hips moving with the horse, her ribcage wide, and her sternum up and lifting toward her chin. The rider can also stretch her arms so they point toward the horse's ears, and then back out to the side. A variation is to have the rider reach gently down with one hand and place it behind her thigh, straighten up again, and put her other hand just behind the opposite thigh and below the saddle panel on the outside.

Bicycle and Frog

Leg exercises without stirrups allow the rider to feel the swinging, independent hip. An exercise that facilitates the so-called following seat involves lifting one knee toward the pommel or horn, lowering it without kicking the horse, and then lifting the other knee. Here the rider will definitely need to hold onto the bucking strap, cantle, or both. If the rider is comfortable, and able to lift one knee at a time, ask her to "ride her bicycle," by lifting one knee, then the other, in time with the horse's trot. This exercise loosens tight flexor tendons and muscles, while reminding the rider that her legs are capable of moving independently.

She can then lift both knees into the frog position as she did in the standstill and the walk—sitting upright without leaning backward. Engaging the abdominal muscles—particularly the lower ones—helps the rider lift and hold the legs as the horse trots. The rider needn't make a big effort here; just a little lift is sufficient. (Only the most athletic and flexible among us are able to sit on just our seat bones and balance on a trotting horse with our knees up high.) One fault to watch out for is the rider falling back behind the vertical. Her back remains in position, with chin up, and hips in line with shoulders.

Lift Off

Is the rider ready for more challenge? If so, ask her to perform a gentle "lift" off the saddle, with one hand on the pommel or horn and the other on the cantle. This requires quite a bit of abdominal strength. Initiate the exercise by tightening and lifting the lower abdominal muscles rather than by pushing with the arms. She needs only to lift an inch or two while keeping the legs very light. Then she can ease (don't thump) back down into the saddle. She can hold the lift for two or three seconds, coming down gently.

Series A
Rising trot
Arms out
Torso turns
Windmills

Series B
Sitting trot
Rising trot
Half seat
Sitting trot
Leg fluff

Series C
(No stirrups, sitting trot)
Bicycle legs
Windmills (alternating)

Series D
(No stirrups, sitting trot)
Hands on head
Hands on belly
Arms out to the side
Arms to the front
Repeat

Series E
Head rolls
Shoulder rolls (from the Walk
    chapter or from Chapter 2)

Chapter 5

Lateral Movements
and Cavalletti on the Longe

Circles on the longe line are wonderful, but sometimes you have to mix it up. The work in this chapter is a bit tougher and requires a little more experience. Experiment with performing lateral movements without the help of the reins—merely using the seat, weight, and legs to move the horse both sideways and forward at the same time.

Lateral at the Walk

As with transitions within and between the gaits, the longeur becomes a passive participant, allowing the rider to control the horse's movements. It helps if you have a horse that knows leg yield and understands cues delivered with clear purpose. Otherwise the horse might react with a "Huh?" and not move at all. Before you do lateral work on the longe line, ride the leg yield movements off the longe line to see how much he knows. A well-trained horse won't need much more than a little seat and leg for a reaction; a less responsive horse may need to be taught the aids for leg yield.

The rider should un-knot the reins if she has them tied up so she can use them during the lateral work to encourage the horse to bend. By the way, transitions within the gaits covered in the last chapter tune the horse to the rider, making this lateral work much easier. I suggest you do those before trying leg yield on the longe.

Leg Yield In

Start at the walk. Pay the line all the way out to create a big circle. The longeur asks the rider to weight her outside seat bone and gently use her outside leg and seat in rhythm with the horse's outside hind leg as it comes forward and pushes against the ground. This is where the earlier exercise, in which we asked the rider to identify which leg was moving, comes in very handy. Ask for only two sideways yet forward steps at first.

Be sure the rider has her hands resting on the saddle, in rein position, or actually holding the reins, adding a slight bend by squeezing the outside rein gently. The rider turns her gaze to the inside of the circle, without collapsing her hip or leaning over the saddle, so the horse feels the subtle shift of the weight signaling him to step to the inside of the circle and cross his legs over. The rider's hips and shoulders remain in line with the horse's shoulders. Many riders want to clamp and pinch the aiding leg. They bring their knees up and tighten their legs. As the longeur, you won't see this on the outside, but watch for it when the pair moves back to the outside track. Beware of that crunching leg and pinching of the rider's own hindquarters.

In the leg yield on the longe, the rider can use her reins to help establish the horse's bend. Even as the horse is stepping sideways toward the center of the circle, the rider's shoulders remain level.

Another step of leg yield. The rider keeps her arms and hands soft and guides the horse toward the center of the circle.

The seat stays relaxed and gently soft, sweeping with the motion of the horse to the side. The leg stays long and "cuddled" around the horse's flank just at the girth, adding pressure in time with the walk step. It might help the rider if the longeur says, "Now, now, now," when it's appropriate to apply leg pressure. The outside leg (in this case, the leg closest to the longeur, because we are moving from outside to inside) stays in contact with the horse; it may need to slide it gently back several inches to keep the horse's hindquarters under control. The horse has to remain tracking forward—if he goes only sideways, he loses all his "umph"; it will be quite difficult for him to move and for the rider to feel the leg yield correctly.

In the leg yield, the rider should have what Susanne von Dietze in *Balance in Motion* calls the rotational seat. Imagine the rider has a pole down her back tied to her spine: as she asks the horse for the sideways movement her hips turn around the pole, gently asking the horse to move in the direction of travel.

After two steps to the inside, the rider can ask the horse to straighten again on the circle by applying both legs and moving the seat more actively forward. The rider must feel the horse resume the circle for several strides, so both rider and horse can become reorganized and the rider can feel the difference between the forward walk, and the forward-and-sideways walk.

Leg Yield Out

Only when the horse is walking forward on the circle should the rider ask the horse to leg yield back out to the larger circle again. Here again, the longeur is passive, guiding the horse around the circle but allowing the rider to do the work. The horse steps across himself, and the longeur watches that the rider remains tall in the saddle, open in the ribcage (no collapsing), long in the leg, and even in the hips.

The longeur will know if the rider is being ineffective with either leg because the horse won't respond correctly. If her outside leg isn't on or if her inside leg is too tense the horse may over bend or ignore the rider. If nothing is happening, try the "less is more" approach: The rider may be trying too hard—tightening her muscles and bones so the horse can't really move at all. The less the rider does, the more carefully the horse listens. Try to have the rider "whisper" the aids rather than shout them. Another potential problem could be that the horse just isn't "sharp" to the aids. You might need to do some transitions to wake him up.

Once you've gotten a couple of good steps in leg yield coming in and going out on the circle, the rider can add more steps, shrinking the circle from fully extended to very small, with some straight-ahead on the circle forward walk steps in between. If all is going well, the longeur gathers the line as the horse comes in, and lets it slide out of her hand as the pair moves out on the circle.

The rider's inside leg and seat bone are working together effectively here, as the horse steps actively sideways and forward.

Leg yielding on the circle is not an easy exercise, so take it one step at a time. It requires patience for the rider and the horse to organize for just one or two steps of leg yield. The confidence the rider has built from the exercises you've worked on until this point are useful for lateral work on the longe line, because a light, free seat and hips, as well as a straight and tall posture and the application of the independent aids are imperative to making this exercise work.

If your rider is confused, she can execute the leg yield one step at a time. The rider presses once with the outside leg, asking for just a single movement toward the inside of the circle. Even the slightest step inside should be rewarded. Watch for rider tilt: many riders confuse a collapsed midsection for an active seat. The space between the ribs and the hips remains even on both sides of the body, and the shoulders stay level. The outside seat bone merely presses slightly toward the opposite leg. Another pitfall is tightness in the hips and thighs. If the rider is stuck or gripping in that "paperclip" fashion we discussed earlier, the horse is less free to step through and use his back effectively. Solve hip and leg tightness using the leg fluff exercise. Have the rider take a stretch break. Do something else for a few minutes until the frustration subsides.

Don't school these leg yields too intensely. The longeur needs to pay attention that the pair remains happy and working. If the horse gets fidgety, go to the trot for a few minutes. If the rider scowls or becomes bossy with her aids, return to a regular walk and do a deep four-count breathing exercise to calm her. You can't accomplish much when horse and rider begin to argue. Remember that horseback riding is one of the hardest sports to do well. It's also highly underappreciated for the physical skill, balance, and sensitivity it takes. It is only after hours in the saddle and an unfortunate few on the ground that we begin to understand how our bodies communicate with our horses.

Lateral work on the longe is where the hooves meet the road, so to speak, because it demands stillness and straightness for the torso with leg and seat activity. The rider has to separate the top, middle, and lower sections of her body and move them independently. Most people can sit the walk like a statue and ride a horse forward while someone else steers. But to move him sideways on a circle requires sitting still, while applying just a little pressure with the seat bone; sitting straight, while directing your focus to the inside or outside of the circle; and finally, using your leg to softly ask the horse to step over without crunching it up or pushing too hard. The move encompasses all that is wonderful and complex about riding, and all we need to do to ride well. Once you've got the calm leg yield going from a large circle to a small one and back again, bravo! It's not an easy task, and the longeur can heap praise on the pair.

LATERAL AT THE TROT

Now try it at the rising trot. Lots of us have a tendency to sit harder and deeper when we're concentrating (or worse yet, make some kind of awful face, stick our tongues out, or bite our lips). This driving seat can inhibit the horse's movement. That's why posting trot is a better way to start practicing trot leg yield, because the rider is off the horse's back 50 percent of the time, and unless the rider is really pounding on the downbeat, her seat will be lighter even when she's in the saddle. The aids remain the same—the leg presses against the horse's side in rhythm with the hind leg stepping forward on the same side. The rider turns her gaze in the direction she wants the horse to travel, adding extra push with the seat bone to make the horse slide right over.

Note the complication with posting on the correct or incorrect diagonal. If the pair is tracking right, but leg yielding off the left leg, have the rider change the diagonal so she's posting with the left leg, *not the right leg*. Whichever side is asking for the leg yield is now considered the *inside* leg, because that's the side the horse is bending around.

The longeur maintains the horse's rhythmic trot, watching the rider for tightness, while gathering up and letting slide the longe line depending on whether the pair is leg yielding to the inside or the outside. And don't forget to change directions—as we've said, every horse and rider have a good side and a bad side, so what you see in the leg yield to the left may not be the same in the leg yield to the right. A rider's drooping left shoulder, for example, has an impact on lateral work in any direction. The tendency is to let the left shoulder drag in the leg yield to the right (from the left driving leg). This confuses any horse that's trying to be accommodating and perform the exercise. You're essentially asking for two things at once. A rider's drooping left shoulder will allow the horse to fall out through his shoulder, making a correct forward and sideways movement very difficult. So keep the rider's posture in mind at all times. It's very easy to get twisted in the leg yield.

Years ago I had no-stirrups lateral-work lessons. My instructor at the time was a Dutch FEI rider for whom I worked in Vermont while I was in college. At first I was fairly intimidated by the idea of leg yield and shoulder-in without stirrups, but as I became more comfortable riding dressage, I realized I was in a much better position riding without stirrups than with them. If your rider is comfortable at the sitting trot and able to keep the horse in a solid trot rhythm without you having to urge the horse on continually (a sign that the horse is either lazy or the rider is too tight in her seat and thigh) you can try a few steps of leg yield at the sitting trot with no stirrups. Riding without stirrups lets the rider focus on keeping her legs long. If she's pinching or gripping she won't be able to stay with the horse's motion; the trot will shorten and the rider will bounce much more intensely. If so, the rider needs to slide her pelvis underneath her spine leaving just a small arch in her back as she moves through the leg yield at the trot. Her hips move gently with the motion.

Shoulder-In

Yes, you can do shoulder-in, even half pass and flying changes on the longe line. But since this book is geared toward everyday riders, not upper level dressage enthusiasts (although all are welcome), instead of a real shoulder-in, we're focusing on a "shoulder-in feel" instead.

In technical terms, the shoulder-in takes place when the horse is slightly crossing his front legs while tracking straight with his hind legs. The horse is bent around the inside leg. A shoulder-in differs from a leg yield because the hind legs continue tracking forward rather than crossing-and-forward. On a longeing circle, the shoulder-in requires a subtle movement of the rider's body toward the inside of the circle. The rider should pick up the reins lightly. She'll hold the outside rein at the horse's neck while asking for the horse to bend by taking a slightly shorter inside rein that directs the horse's shoulders. The longeur may have to signal the horse to keep going forward while she's adding just a little bit of pressure to the line to cue the horse to bend around the rider's inside leg.

The rider steps deeper into the inside stirrup, using the inside leg to create the bend. The rider turns her shoulders and hips slightly toward the inside of the circle, thereby directing the horse to move his own shoulders in the same direction. The aids are similar to the leg yield. The rider's inside leg directs the horse at the girth while her outside leg holds the horse's haunches tracking forward. Just a feeling of bringing the shoulders off the track is all that's needed.

If the rider becomes intense and clamped, try this without stirrups and at the walk first. The rider will have less opportunity to brace her leg and will ride with a longer leg without her stirrups. If the horse doesn't respond, he may not understand the rider's aids. The longeur can come out from middle of the circle, take a light hold of both reins near the bit, and ask the horse for the inside bend. The shoulder-in is difficult for most horses because it requires them to step under with their inside hind legs—and that's a level of strength that's achieved over time, not in one longeing session.

Poles and Cavalletti

More advanced work with rhythm, half halts, and the half seat can be added by putting poles on the ground. The cavalletti work described here assumes the horse is experienced with trotting poles and won't jump or stumble through them. He should be trained so he maintains a steady trot rhythm all the way through, no matter how many poles you lay down. Otherwise, cavalletti work turns into a dangerous mess of hooves and poles. The longeur needs to have control of the horse and be able to regulate his trot through the poles correctly. Doing cavallettis while on the longe lets the rider feel a rhythmic, suspended trot, and gives her an opportunity to control the pace and size of the horse's steps with her seat and leg. The longeur can help, of course, but it's best to let the rider figure it out on her own.

Set a single pole on the circle and ask the pair to approach it at the posting trot. Maintain the rhythm around the circle by using a quick, light tug on the line to slow the horse down if he's getting too rushed, or a little encouragement with the whip if he's too slow. Even and steady is the name of this game, and that's the longeur's responsibility in the beginning of this exercise. Note that the horse's rhythm shouldn't change *over the pole*, but can adjust before it to meet it in stride. He can change his rhythm three or four strides before the pole. The rider keeps her eyes up and forward at all times, watching the world through the horse's ears. She shouldn't look at the ground or at the pole (a very common fault), or even too far ahead on the circle. The gaze should be just a stride or two beyond where the horse and rider are. If she's looking halfway across the circle, she could be turning her body too much. The horse will feel her looking ahead and may speed up in response.

Once the rider has trotted over the pole several times at the posting trot, she takes the half seat, or, if she's in a dressage or Western saddle, a lighter seat, a few strides before the pole. Even if you're longeing in a Western saddle, the rider can step deeper into her stirrups, lift her seat above the saddle and bend slightly forward. I call it an "almost-half seat" because the

Practicing half seat around the entire circle.

longer stirrups of the Western or dressage saddle preclude the rider from executing a true two-point—her seat may actually touch the saddle lightly. In the almost-half seat, or "three-point," because two legs and the seat connect to the horse, the rider's body is more upright than the 45 degree angle of the true two-point. Maintain the lighter seat for a few strides after the pole. Then the rider can return to a balanced and rhythmic posting trot for a few strides before taking her half seat again.

The third level of this exercise involves the rider hold-

Begin with one pole ridden at the half seat until the rider gets the feeling of how the horse will actively lift and push with his hindquarters.

Two poles ridden at the sitting trot help the rider learn to swing through her hips.

ing the half seat all the way around the circle. If she's feeling secure and her heels are well down and calves stretched long, ask her to put her arms out to the side as if she's flying over the pole. This requires the rider work on a long leg that is directly underneath her. Anything less and she'll either fall backwards or forwards. If she loses her balance, she can return to the posting trot. Over time the rider will be able to balance over the pole in half seat. The rider can put one hand on the horse's neck for support. The longeur guides the horse on a straight line through the center of the pole. Add another single pole, placing it 4'3" to 4'6" from the first pole, depending on your horse's stride. A large-strided horse needs more space, but you can ask a short-strided horse to lift and push a little more by widening the space between the poles a couple of inches. The wider cavalletti cause the horse's step to become more elevated over the poles, and the rider may become unbalanced or surprised by the amount of airtime that requires.

The rider should do the two-pole exercise in rising trot with stirrups first so she can get the feeling of staying in the air a fraction of a second longer. The longeur keeps the horse trotting steadily along, allowing him to adjust his stride before the poles. Most horses will do so. Of course, those that have never trotted cavalletti before may look at them, or leap over them, so inexperienced horses should probably not be used for this particular exercise until they've practiced off the longe line, then on the longe line with no rider aboard.

While the pair trots the poles, the longeur needs to watch for common faults: posting over the cavalletti pinpoints whether a rider uses her toes or knees to grip, or falls forward or backward while posting, or posts with an uneven rhythm. A couple of poles on the ground will magnify those problems.

If the rider keeps her legs long, stretched, and underneath herself during the "up" phase of the rising trot, she'll be able to maintain her trot rhythm. But riders who post from their toes instead of their calf muscles exaggerate the "up" of the post when the horse takes a bigger step. They'll point their toes down and heave themselves out of the saddle, often getting behind the vertical (or "left behind" as it's sometimes called) on the downbeat. The post over the poles isn't higher, but rather the "up" beat is slightly longer. Also, the rider should be able to feel the horse's thrust, and should use the thrust to help lift her out of the saddle. The up movement should be fairly effortless, without exaggeration, heaving, or bouncing. The poles can help the rider feel the horse push—then the rider can work on the gentle post without the poles for the rest of the circle.

Working over the poles, the rider can bring her arms out to the side, to her waist, over her head, behind her back, and to the rein position. Ask the rider to post over the poles, putting her hands out to the side two strides before the first pole. The exercise, which will help the rider and the longeur develop an "eye" for the horse's stride, comes from an old jumping exercise that involves actually seeing where the horse will lift off for a jump long before the point of takeoff, and counting down the strides. At first we'd start off on a straight line: eight, seven, six . . . to takeoff. If the horse changed his rhythm, we'd either get a long or short distance to the jump. But if we kept the same pace all the way down the line, we'd lift off the ground when we reached "one." At first we missed every time, but with some practice we soon could see the lift-off point from halfway around the arena. Even if you have absolutely no interest in jumping, the pole exercise can help develop a feel for a horse's pace and how it affects his footfalls and rhythm.

Variations on the two-pole exercise involve having the rider close her eyes and continue posting through the poles to feel the horse lifting his legs up and over. A rider with good feel can be asked to count down the strides and say "now" just as she approaches the poles. Have the rider practice the exercise first with eyes open, then close them about three strides from the poles and count down, "Three-two-one."

When the rider's eye has developed enough to see the takeoff point three strides away, the rider can take the half-seat position from that point, crossing her arms in front of her. She says out loud, "Three, two, one." Have the rider find the point even if you can see it very clearly. Later you can add another stride, having her rise into half-seat with arms crossed four strides from the pole, then five strides.

A third method is to have the rider keep her arms out to the side while in half-seat position, and then return to the sitting trot afterwards. The sequence is (1) sitting trot on the circle; (2) half seat three strides out; (3) arms out to the side one stride out; (4) back to sitting trot afterwards. For the rider to manage all these movements, plus allow her hips and seat to move freely in the sitting trot, demands quickness. She may feel really awkward, but later she'll develop ease in the transitions from position to position. Changing positions rapidly develops hands, seat, and legs that move independently. It forces the rider to think about timing. Add up to five poles in a row, angling them around the circle so that the longeur can reel the horse in a step or two for a shorter stride, or reel him out for a longer stride. Work the poles in all three rider positions—posting, half seat, and sitting. Add arm challenges, such as arms out to the side, in front, and crossed over the chest. A fairly confident rider who can work well at the sitting trot should able to ride the poles without stirrups.

For another variation you can place a set of two poles on one side of the circle and another set of two on the other side. The rider remains in rising trot while the longeur aims the horse for the center of each set of poles. The rider can use the same set of exercises. Counting down strides; changing between sitting, posting, and half-seat; and varying the position of the arms all become more challenging with the addition of another set of poles. The extra set of poles helps the rider develop her eye and timing.

Series A
  Spiral out, four steps leg yield
  Spiral in, four steps leg yield

Series B
  Spiral out, two steps leg yield
  Straighten
  Shoulder-in feel, quarter of a
    circle

Series C
  Three poles: Sitting trot
  Three poles: Sitting trot, half
    seat arms out three strides
    before the poles, over the
    poles
  Return to sitting trot one stride
    after poles

Series D
  Half seat, full circle, over the
    poles
  Canter, quarter circle, return to
    trot before the poles
  Trot poles

Chapter 6
Cantering On

Once the rider is comfortable and able to sit deeply yet lightly in sitting trot, trot over poles, and move confidently from full seat to half seat and back again without using the reins for balance, it's time to add some transitions between trot and canter.

Relaxing the Tense Rider

Even though a collected, controlled canter is really no faster than a forward trot, some people fear it. The gait feels intimidating, especially if the rider has had a bad experience at some point in her riding career. Perhaps she was on a trail ride and the horse raced for home and she fell off, or perhaps she's just a fearful person overall who is using the longe work to build her confidence. Take baby steps with the unconfident rider. Don't attempt the canter if the horse isn't quiet and obedient.

Ironically, many riders find the canter easier than the trot, because the gait is smoother. The longeur may want to remind the rider that a well-trained horse doesn't actually speed up that much in the canter, he just changes the rhythm and order of his footfalls. Some horses *have* been taught that canter means go faster; others canter so slowly they're dragging their hooves. Either way, if the horse isn't cantering with clear beats at a reasonable, rather than rushing, rhythm, the rider is going to have a hard time feeling comfortable.

To prepare for the trot-canter transition, the rider may want to pick up the reins to feel more secure. Her hands should be low and quiet and, if it's possible to do so without slumping, she can rest them on the horse's neck. Typically, when a tense rider asks for a canter transition, she will close her thighs and grip her legs tightly around the horse. This pushes the rider down

One way for a nervous rider to feel more secure at the canter is to put one hand on the cantle and one on the pommel. Then she can switch.

on the horse's spine and makes it difficult for him to arch his back and step underneath himself, which is necessary for the canter transition. Instead of jumping smoothly into the canter, the horse trots really fast. The rider grips tighter and the horse trots faster yet. The rider starts bouncing and loses her seat. To avoid this unpleasant scenario, ask the rider to take a really deep exhaling breath just as you (as the longeur), say the word "canter." The rider applies her inside leg at the girth while her outside leg nudges just behind the girth. The exhaling exercise naturally relaxes the rider's tension—the rider can't exhale and remain tense.

For the first few strides of the canter, ask only that the rider sweep her seat and become comfortable with the rhythm. It's okay to hold the bucking strap or horn. If the horse is in a good rhythm and the rider is comfortably swinging and following with her seat, ask her to raise the inside hand in the air to stretch her body and release even more tension she might be holding in her ribs and upper chest, helping the rider grow taller. She will become more even in her seat. After a stride or two, she can switch to the outside hand, which will assure she isn't leaning to the inside. At the canter, riders can easily build a habit of leaning over the horse instead of helping the horse by riding with level hips and shoulders. A balanced rider aids the horse's balance, too. He can more easily "stand up" underneath the rider, rather than "motorcycling"—falling in—around the circle.

Once she's comfortable with both hands off the bucking strap and reins (tie them back up if necessary) and can raise her hands individually, the rider places both hands on her waist. Here she can feel the horse swinging and what affect that movement has on her midsection. She should grow tall and light, as if she's polishing the saddle lightly with the seat of her pants. Her inside hip follows the horse's shoulder around the circle, helping him to stay on the circumference. The inside hip is ever-so-slightly more active than the outside hip.

Identifying Rider Faults

The longeur can often feel the rider's faults through the longe line. If the rider falls in, the horse may react by letting his shoulder fall out, making it difficult for the longeur to keep the horse on the circle. If you, as the longeur, feel more pressure on the longe line, you should ask the rider if her feet are evenly weighted in the stirrups and if her seat bones are level. The rider may need to momentarily step into the outside stirrup. If it happens again, it's likely your rider is tilted.

Another common fault is a locked inside hip. Instead of following the motion of the inside foreleg as it comes up and strikes the ground, the hip has become tight and inhibits the horse's ability to turn on the circle. While the rider's seat swings, her upper body should remain tall and stable. If the horse continually breaks to a strung out, downhill trot, the rider may be holding too much with her seat, gripping with her inner thighs, or acciden-tally executing a half-halt (a brief moment of holding that signals the horse that another cue is about to be given). In that case, the rider is tight some-where in her back or seat.

Several different solutions work for the locked-up canter seat. The easiest involves asking the rider to activate and swing her inside hip more vigorously. She may need to exaggerate that motion. Tight shoulders or a locked back could also be the culprit. Ask the rider to roll her shoulders, alternating left and right while the horse canters, allowing her to open her chest, lift her sternum, and grow taller to release and lighten the seat.

Hands Behind the Saddle

Now ask the rider to put both hands behind the saddle, resting them gently on the panels just behind each thigh. We did this exercise at the trot, but at different gaits the exercise offers something new. At the canter, placing the hands behind the body draws the shoulders back and down gently along the

Although this photo shows the hands behind the saddle exercise at the trot, the same idea applies at the canter. The hands resting behind the thighs put the shoulders in the proper position.

spine and pushes the seat gently forward toward the pommel. In this position, it is nearly impossible to slump or fall forward. Riders who tense at the canter want to "curl" toward their centers. Placing the hands behind her counteracts that posture. It allows the rider to focus on her following seat, which moves with the horse quietly. It also ceases the pumping of the shoulders, which is a common canter fault. If all is going well, the rider appears quite still and graceful.

Leg Fluffs

The uptight rider will benefit from breathing exercises and leg fluffs in concert. Ask the rider to open her legs out and away from the saddle with each exhale. The count would be: "Exhale, two-three, inhale, two-three," and with each breath out the rider softens and lengthens her legs, bringing them out, back, and down into position.

Exhaling through Transitions

For the rider who is still not quite comfortable cantering, the longeur should ask the horse for a steady, rhythmic trot. The rider can sit or post the trot, however she's most comfortable. The longeur asks the rider for several long and deep breaths in and out within the trot rhythm. Continue the rhythmic breathing, and at the same time ask the rider to use the soft gaze or third eye that we talked about in the chapter on working at the standstill. We're asking the rider to open her range of vision from a directed point on the circle to more peripheral gaze.

When the rider is ready, the longeur counts the inhales and exhales as she asks the horse to canter. This exercise gives the rider and horse the feeling that the canter departure is no big deal. Not much changes from the canter to the trot—the rider can consider the canter a trot with a different rhythm. However, a speeding up trot-into-canter isn't acceptable. The horse should step quietly from the rhythmic trot to the rhythmic canter. If he doesn't, the longeur needs to contemplate why. Is the rider gripping? Is the horse upset about something? Or is he just not well schooled? Whatever the reason, bring the horse back to a controlled trot right away and start again. Don't let the horse run into the canter from the trot.

Once you've gotten the canter, and the rider is comfortable, continue for three or four strides. Then return to trot in a balanced fashion. Repeat the exercise, giving the rider time to collect herself. Go back and forth between canter and trot until the transition becomes smooth. You can frame this exercise as a transition practice session, rather than a cantering practice session. In each of these transitions, the rider should maintain her upright, tall body position. The rider who falls either forward or backward needs a stronger core to hold her tall. The longeur can stress the tall spine and deep breathing to keep the rider's body tuned in with the horse's as he changes his gait from three beats to two beats and back again.

Bucking Strap

Here's another tip on building confidence in the canter: The rider is encouraged to use the bucking strap to help her feel secure but with this caveat: she should not be holding so hard that she's forcing her seat down into the saddle. Not only is this driving seat incorrect, it's uncomfortable for the horse. If she must hold on, she should do so with a light hand. And as she becomes more confident at the canter, she can lighten her grip on the strap until she is just barely touching it. A rider who slumps as a reaction to anxiety should hold onto the saddle's cantle with the inside hand. This will force her to keep her body turning on the circle. The cantle handhold will demand the rider bring her shoulders back behind her, keeping her upright. The rider belongs in this position in the downward transition to trot as well. When the horse dives downward during the transition instead of floating into the trot, it unbalances both horse and rider.

Soft Palate

Another interesting exercise to turn the focus away from tension at the canter is to explore the soft palate as we did at the walk and trot. As the rider is cantering along, ask her to slide her tongue gently along the roof of her mouth until she feels the change in texture that occurs toward the back of the throat. Looking for the soft palate with the tongue aligns the head on the neck in the proper position. This exercise is especially useful for riders who have "duck head," where they stick their necks out over their chests, or for those that look down. If the rider can't find the soft palate, chances are she is bending her neck bending incorrectly. She will also find that it's much easier to find the soft palate if she's relaxed. Ask your rider to smile! Tension in the neck, a stern angry face, or a spine out of alignment in any way will likely prevent the rider from finding that soft spot in her mouth.

A Final Note on Relaxation

Don't go on to any of the exercises that follow if the rider is uncomfortable cantering, holds her breath, becomes tense, or holds with her thighs or knees. There is plenty to work on, and many ways to relax the tense rider using some of the exercises discussed in the walk and trot chapters. They can all be applied easily here. Some particularly useful ones are:

Windmills at the canter test the rider's balance and ability to swing through her hips.

- Holding the arms out to the side and turning gently from inside to outside.

- Closing the eyes for half a circle.
- Changing from half seat to full seat.

FOOTFALLS

Identifying the canter's footfalls is another way to take a rider's mind off her fear while developing her sensitivity. At first, have the rider identify the horse's front inside foreleg (his leading leg) as it strikes the ground. Then add the other two beats by saying, "Front, two, three, pause; front, two, three, pause." You can also focus on identifying just the hind inside leg strike off, which is useful when the rider is working on timing for the canter depart or practicing flying lead changes. The rider says "now" when the inside hind strikes off the ground. Accomplished equestrian and author Jane Savoie uses this method to instruct riders when to apply the flying change aid.

Once the rider can do so with her eyes open and she fully understands the footfalls of the canter, ask her to do it with her eyes closed, identifying the inside hind as it strikes off and the foreleg as it strikes the ground. This exercise is useful for educating a rider to the feel of the canter, while less experienced riders can use their newly gained knowledge of the canter footfalls to tell whether the horse is "four-beating"—cantering not forward enough—so it feels more like four beats instead of three. Another way to use the gait-identifying exercise is to help rider clearly identify on which lead the horse is cantering.

HALF SEAT, FULL SEAT

Another confidence-building exercise is to have the rider move into the half-seat position. Even in a dressage saddle or Western saddle where the rider's stirrups may be quite long, she can work in the half-seat position, supporting herself gently with her calf muscles and letting her legs lengthen into the stirrups. The half-seat position can be maintained for an entire circle of canter, with the seat centered over the legs. The rider who is ready to return to the seated position does so softly, using her abdominal muscles and a strong back to ease into the saddle again.

The longeur may need to ask the rider to readjust her seat, scooping her pelvis under her hips again. Then the rider can repeat the half-seat, full-seat transition, spending three strides in each position and practicing balance in both. Don't forget to ask the rider if she's breathing. Riders sometimes hold their breath when they're concentrating. It's also your responsibility to see that the rider's leg stays in position and does not swing back behind her in the half seat (which will throw off her balance) or out in front of her, putting the rider in a "chair seat," as if she were reclining in a chair rather than sitting tall in the saddle. Switching can help the rider become more confident by allowing her to realize the wide range of motion she has in all three gaits. There is benefit for the horse with the half-seat, full-seat exercise. He has an opportunity to stretch his back muscles and relax into the canter. If you are using side reins (see Chapter 1 on equipment) the horse can stretch deeply into the contact they create with the bit.

Posting to the Canter

After a few rounds of half-seat, full-seat canter, the rider should try "posting to the canter." Because it's a three-beat gait with a moment of suspension, the rider can easily find a posting rhythm, although it's different from the one-two, up-down trot. Just gradually decrease the amount of time the rider spends in the saddle during the half-seat, full-seat. The longeur can count "up" for two strides, "down" for one stride. The time between "up" and "down" will be longer than in the trot.

Posting to the canter makes the rider more coordinated, able to go from half seat to full seat quickly and easily. It can be a good way to gently warm up the cold-backed horse who may be unable to handle the weight and pressure of the rider's full seat first thing on a winter morning. Plus it adds variety to the canter work. This exercise is a good way to keep a horse that tends to speed up in check, because the rider keeps the rhythm steady by creating it with her post.

Transitions within the Gait

Just as the rider varied the trot pace using only her seat and leg, we can do the same with the canter. In the posting canter, the rider gently closes her thighs as she eases back to the saddle to slow the rhythm. This is a very gentle movement—almost imperceptible. If this seems like too much for your rider to manage, ask her to return to the seated canter, scooping her seat and fluffing her legs so she can open her pelvis and allow the horse's back to come up, under, and through in the canter. While maintaining the rhythm of the horse's steady one-two-three-pause, have the rider gently hold her seat and sink into the center a little more deeply to shorten the horse's stride. The rider does most of the work while the longeur remains passive. If the horse isn't reacting, the rider might need to take a little squeeze of the reins.

The longeur can help the rider by reminding the horse with a little more hold on the longe line, in time with the rider's aid, that he needs to listen to the rider. Often when the rider pinches too much with her upper thighs, the horse either ignores her or speeds up. So the rider has to be both quick and subtle with her demand; just a quick inner thigh squeeze and hold, while at the same time applying a little leg pressure to keep the horse from stopping altogether. We're asking for only a smaller stride, not a trot or a walk. If the horse slows down too much the first few times, he's only reacted to the rider's request. She should lighten the aids a bit each time to see how gentle she can be and still get a response.

The point of this canter exercise is to keep the rhythm steady—the rider can count it out as part of the eyes-closed exercise. She can use the seat to ask the horse to lengthen the stride and then shorten it again, but while the *length* of the stride may change, the rhythm does not. This is fairly advanced work and might not be achievable for all horse and rider pairs right away. It may take practice off the longe to show the horse and rider what you mean.

BIG AND BOUNDING

Next up on the canter roster are the more defined transitions within the gait.

First check the rider's position:

- Legs underneath her properly?
- Head and neck well aligned?
- Hands quiet and calm in rein position, following the movement of the horse's neck?
- Upper body quiet and strong, shoulder blades back and down gently?
- Ask the rider for a gentle leg fluff to make sure she's not gripping with her thighs and knees.

To do transitions within the canter, from a working canter with a good rhythm to a more active canter and back again, the longeur must be well in control of the horse; he should be obedient and listening to both the longeur and the rider. Begin by having the rider sit the canter without giving any aids. The longeur asks the horse to canter forward a little more strongly with a voice aid or a little encouragement from the longe whip. The canter stride should lengthen, but not necessarily become faster, although it may feel that way to the rider. After a few strides the longeur takes a little more hold of the line for a step or two to ask the horse again to shorten his stride. Repeat this a few times, asking the horse to go forward and collect at the canter. The rider's seat follows the motion as the horse engages and pushes over his back, then she shortens her hip swing to ask the horse to shorten his stride.

If the horse feels ready to try it without the help of the longeur, the rider can then ask for the collected and extended canter. The longeur directs the rider at which point in the circle to ask for the bigger canter and at which point to slow the canter. That way the rider can prepare both herself and the horse with a gentle half-halt just before giving the cues. Depending on the horse and the rider, it sometimes takes a few strides to get a reaction. To ask for the lengthening canter the longeur lets the horse canter on a slightly bigger circle, if possible. The rider just holds with her seat for a step or two—not much, though, because a sensitive horse would likely break to trot—and then applies her leg aids in one quick step to ask the horse to canter on. The rider's seat must remain relaxed, and she shouldn't pump with her upper body.

In fact, it may be useful for the rider to try the first few transitions within the canter gaits in half seat. Some horses know this as a cue to go forward. Better to practice this way than to allow the rider to busily kick with her legs and push with her seat. The longeur needs to watch the rider to make sure her legs don't swing out behind her in half seat. Her back is flat and her half seat is a little more upright than the 45 degrees described earlier. The longeur can allow the horse to move out a bit here, and even encourage it.

When the horse is really stepping forward the rider can gently return to the seated upright position. The rider slows the horse's pace by holding her body and hips and slowing the motion, gently closing the thighs. There's a fine line here between closing the thighs and gripping with the thigh. It's an important distinction: A gently closing thigh communicates to the horse that the rider wants him to move a certain direction. A closing thigh slows the motion, putting gentle pressure on the horse's back muscles that run from his hindquarters; it can also be used to ask the horse to turn or move laterally. A gripping thigh, on the other hand, inhibits the horse's movement—stopping the flow of energy over the back and to the neck, and making it difficult for the horse to continue cantering. The rider's gripping thighs will pop her up and out of the saddle, causing a cascading set of problems from a hunched back to a forward upper body to ineffective leg aids. Once the rider is back down in the seat, she should move her legs out and back, away from the saddle, to free and loosen her thighs.

As the rider becomes comfortable with the half seat, the longeur asks the horse to bound forward in the canter while the rider remains seated. She should ask for a bigger stride, not a gallop or an out of control canter. The rider, while seated, lightens her lower body by putting a few ounces of pressure into both stirrups at the same moment the horse pushes off for the extended canter. It is a common rider fault to sink into the saddle and push with the seat to increase the canter stride.

If you are longeing on the right lead, the right hip comes slightly forward as the horse's right front leg comes forward. The rider's upper body follows the arc of the circle, without exaggerating it or leaning inward. With the bigger canter, the rider swings more with the inside hip; to shorten the canter the rider holds with the inside hip to slow the motion. As the rider becomes more adept at controlling the pace at the canter, the longeur cues the horse less and less. The rider asks the horse to step forward at the moment of spring by applying her leg for a moment and swinging actively yet lightly with her seat. As you practice this exercise you'll also find an added benefit: The horse will become more responsive and light. It will become easier and easier to "play" with the different canters—big and bounding or more collected.

ARMS AND BELLIES

At the center you can practice all the same arm exercises we did at the walk and trot. I re-emphasize that the longeing horse needs to be quiet and consistent at the canter, maintaining his rhythm.

One of the best canter seat correction exercises is to work with the inside hand resting on the lower back, just below the natural arch and just above the sacrum (the flat plate that is between the pelvis joints). The outside hand rests on the rider's belly. This hand position places the rider so her shoulders and hips are following the horse's shoulders (which should be in line) and the rider and horse are following the arc of the circle. The rider holds her chin up and lets her shoulder blades come together along her back. With each stride she scoops her pelvis gently into the hand on her stomach. Next, the rider places her inside hand in the air and stretches up through her fingertips and down through her toes.

She switches arms next, putting the inside hand on the stomach and the outside hand behind the back. By doing so, the rider feels over-rotated to the outside of the circle. This position has an impact on the horse's balance. For example, if he tends to drag the outside shoulder to the outside of the circle, putting pressure on the longe line, rotating to the outside mimics what would be necessary to achieve counter-flexion. This helps straighten

Placing her hands on her lower back and lower stomach at the canter helps the rider feel the movement of her body in relationship to the canter.

the horse and bring his body to a level position, with his outside shoulder on the circle rather than falling out. The longeur can help by lightly tugging on the longe line and adding a little whip activity simultaneously. Another reason to rotate to the outside of the circle is to give the rider a feel of proper position on the circle.

Stepping deeply into the outside stirrup is another way to bring the horse's shoulder back into alignment. The exercise also straightens the rider who leans too much to the inside, or collapses her outside shoulder while overcompensating for the open ribcage we created in the previous exercise.

To vary the exercise, the rider switches hands from her back to her stomach with each stride. She may even add a little pressure on her stomach while she's doing so. The pressing action encourages the rider to lift her stomach and tuck her pelvis during the "pause" beat of the canter. The physical movement of changing the hands accompanies an inhale breath to give the rider a sense of lightness and openness in the chest as the horse jumps through to the next canter stride. This is a good exercise to improve flying lead changes because the rider feels how to change her position slightly for the new lead before the moment of the actual lead change.

Now the rider can swim with her arms, raising each one over her head and forward toward the horse's ear, then returning her arm deliberately to rein position. The longeur keeps the canter circle large and the horse coming forward in a lively pace, so the rider won't be distracted with maintaining the canter. The rider's hips need to continue to swing and follow the canter stride.

TRANSITIONS WITHOUT STIRRUPS

More advanced canter exercises—transition exercises between the trot and the canter without stirrups—involve good timing and a strong position. A horse that falls into the trot and then sprawls out trotting fast will teach the rider to sit up and hold with her seat to keep from bouncing out of the saddle. The same is true with the upward transition, which we did earlier with stirrups. A horse that runs into the canter needs to be collected gently before the rider asks for the depart, and the timing of the transition is important to get a smooth lift-off.

The rider drops her stirrups and crosses them over the horse's withers so they don't bang against his sides. She remains passive and relaxed, legs long and open, the first few times the longeur asks for the canter. The horse should respond quickly and cleanly. If he runs into the canter, the rider may be gripping. The

Transitions between trot and canter (here demonstrated without stirrups) build confidence.

longeur's timing for the cue could have been incorrect, unbalancing the horse. Working without stirrups, the rider should feel free to hold onto the bucking strap or horn lightly, but not so intensely that she's grinding her seat into the saddle by simultaneously pulling up.

A lot of riders find the canter without stirrups much easier to sit than the trot—and it's usually a smoother, more pleasant gait. When the rider is comfortable, the longeur can begin to ask her to do some exercises with her feet, since we worked on her arms when she had her stirrups. The leg should be held lightly in position. A gripping leg can be fixed by imagining that each leg is a beanbag; firm, steady, but malleable. In the canter without stirrups, ask the rider to softly point her toes up, and then down, and then back to neutral. If all is going well, ask the rider to circle each foot, concentrating on keeping the leg long without banging the horse's flanks. Circling the feet at the canter gives a rider the feeling of wrapping her leg down and long around the horse, and how it would feel to keep her heel away from the horse's side except when he needs to be reminded to go forward. Circling the heels is a good antidote to the nagging leg that riders with lazy horses tend to develop. It's also good practice for riders who'd like to wear spurs because it builds leg and heel control. Once the rider has circled both ankles individually, she can circle them at the same time.

CANTERING FROGS AND BICYCLES

Since hip mobility is such a crucial part of riding, I like to work on it in all gaits. Keep the horse's canter rhythmic and forward, and ask the rider to hold the inside hand on the bucking strap or horn. Then ask her to contract her lower abdominals to raise her inside leg up from the knee as far as possible. This is what I like to call the "half frog," as opposed to the frog we did at the trot and the walk. The rider leans just a little behind the vertical line if necessary, but ideally she'll stay on the triangle of her seat.

This exercise not only takes coordination and abdominal strength, it takes a good longeur to keep the horse going. A horse that feels the uneven seat pressure might be tempted to stop, but the longeur should encourage the horse to keep cantering. Any small attempt at half frog is a good effort. If your rider doesn't have the flexibility of a gymnast, just have her lift as much as she can, hold for a couple of seconds, and then *slowly* release, unfurling the strings of her abdominal and thigh muscles. If she's holding on with her outside hand, she can use the inside hand to gently raise her thigh a bit more.

Do this exercise tracking in both directions, as with all the exercises, so the longeur can see that the rider isn't gripping with the opposite leg or holding on tightly with her heel. If you feel the horse speed up, use your gentling voice to keep him calm and steady in the canter. If the rider gets the feeling of separating her hips and raising one leg, she can do the bicycle exercise at the canter, raising one leg and then the other. It can be a small lift rather than an effort that upsets the centered body. If the rider starts falling backwards, direct her to relax and recenter before starting the exercise again.

CARRYING THE EGGS

Practicing quiet, following hands on the longe line gives the rider a true feeling of independence of the different parts of the body. Remember your childhood egg-and-spoon relay race? We focused on keeping that hand carrying the egg still with the utmost concentration. A similar attention to the hands and rein position helps the rider become more sensitive to the bit and contact with the horse. Quiet hands are vital to becoming a good rider—it's cruel to pull on the horse's mouth. Imagine yourself with a piece of metal in your mouth and a rider pulling and bouncing along. Not fun, and certainly not kind. That's why rein exercises have to be really gentle and correct.

Riders have different lengths in their upper and lower arms. So, too, do horses have different neck lengths. I struggled with this personally with my 17-hand, long-as-a-snake thoroughbred. I was a chronic slumper, partially but not wholly because I have short arms and he was difficult to collect. But something was wrong with my riding—not the length of my arms or the size of my horse. At the time my instructor felt it was the length of my horse's neck. "You need a smaller horse," she would say. Now I know better—I didn't need a smaller horse, I needed longe lessons.

A correct rein is always steady, soft, and elastic. At the canter, the contact follows the motion of the horse's neck ever so slightly as it moves up, out, and forward. The hands and arms follow so the horse can easily use his neck to balance himself. Because the horse is constantly readjusting his balance in the canter, you can't hold the reins in a static position, because the horse will ultimately bump into the bit.

To teach rein position in the canter and to develop a good feel of the correct contact, ask the rider to uncross and pick up her stirrups again (you can work on this without stirrups later) and go into her two-point position. Have her place her hands on either side of the horse's neck just forward of the withers, on the front edge of each shoulder. She should keep her strong, flat-backed half-seat position. Canter around twice to give the rider the opportunity to feel the horse's neck moving up, out, and down. Then have her gently return to seated position without moving her hands. She'll need to open her elbows quite a bit, but her hands stay in place. The rider should feel the steady, yet elastic contact that's necessary to develop educated, gentle hands. The elbows open and close, open and close, with each stride of the canter.

If you have a short jumping crop, you can have the rider use it to keep the arms and hands even steadier (imagine two eggs and two spoons). Return to the walk and hand the rider the crop, without startling the horse. Have her place the crop parallel to the ground just in front of the pommel and have her hold the crop, an end in each hand, while the longeur asks the horse to canter. As the rider gains her seat and begins to follow the rhythm of the canter, have her lift the crop an inch or two above the withers where the reins would normally be. She can practice the following motion of the reins at canter by keeping the crop level and sliding her arms gently forward and back with the motion of the horse.

Now try the trot-canter transitions again, with stirrups, as the rider moves the crop to mimic the rein position during the transition. Her hands should remain softly still, with the outside hand in front of the inside hand, mimicking the arc of the circle and the arch of the horse's body as he bends around the turn. However, if the rider was holding the reins instead of the crop, she might need to shorten her inside rein just a little bit for a correct bend. As the horse trots, the rider's elbows open and close with the post. At the moment of transition from trot to canter, any tension on the reins inhibits the horse's natural gait and causes him to tighten. The crop follows the reaching movement of the horse's neck as he steps forward into the canter. The longeur watches for the rider's hands to become bouncy or for her shoulders to come forward.

The same exercise can be done without crops, of course. It's just a matter of being able to hold the hands steady in all three gaits. Another option is to have your rider hook her pinky fingers under the bucking strap for steadiness if necessary, thumbs turned up. Or she can work the exercise without any props, focusing on keeping a following motion with the hands and arms without looking down at them. The longeur serves as the rider's eyes in this case, telling her to steady her hands, bring them up or down, or relax her elbows. Some riders over-flex their wrists or flatten their hands rather than carrying them in the thumbs-up position. The longeur corrects these faults with verbal cues while the rider continues looking up and riding forward. In the trot-to-canter transition, it's especially important for the rider's hands and arms to stay soft. Riders who fear the canter may hold the reins too tightly in the transition, inhibiting the horse's motion. The longeur can watch for this during the transition, telling the rider to "give the reins"—even if she's only holding imaginary ones—at the moment of lift-off.

TORSO AND ARMS

Now the rider can experiment with moving her body in different directions at the canter. She holds her arms to the side and turns her torso to the outside of the circle. The rider and the longeur can communicate about how the horse feels as the rider shifts her weight to her outside seat bone. The rider slowly turns her torso to the inside. How does the gait (with the inside seat bone strongly weighted) feel to the longeur? Each change in body position may change the horse's canter a little, and the longeur should be able to feel this ever so slightly in the hand that's holding the longe line.

Arms taut, the rider stretches up and lightens her seat at the canter.

The rider stretches tall from the saddle, bringing her hands straight in the air overhead. She keeps the arms taut and the legs long and under her hips. Have her stretch up and keep "sweeping" the seat by stepping down in the stirrups while stabilizing the upper body with her hands overhead. The rider should feel the swing of the canter coming through her lower body. Now have the rider bring her arms out to the side again, and then behind her back. The longeur should tell the rider how and when to do each movement, by saying, "Up, side, back; up, side back."

Working through these canter exercises will help even the most timid rider gain confidence at this gait. Although some riders are intimidated by what feels like a faster gait, the longeur can remind the rider that the canter is sometimes easier to sit than the trot. Additionally, once the rider becomes confident cantering, all kinds of possibilities open up to them—from cantering on the trail to jumping.

Chapter 7
JUMPING

Learning to jump on the longe line is a lot of fun and is a great confidence builder for any rider—even a Western rider who might encounter a log or a ditch on trail rides. I believe that being able to ride a horse over a jump is a fundamental riding skill, even if you never plan to jump a course or gallop around the Rolex three-day event cross country course. In many situations riding over a jump is a necessity—a downed tree in the trail or a horse that jumps over roots. Dressage riders can jump their horses for a change of pace. Western riders might have to pop a jump in a trail class. And sometimes jumping might be just for kicks.

Half-seat practice at the trot to prepare for jumping. The rider is resting her hands on the horse's neck and her elbows are bent.

First, have the rider shorten her stirrups so her center of gravity is just a little further forward in the saddle and she's able to raise her body out of the saddle and into half seat more easily. Then do the exercises in this chapter on trotting over poles.

TROTTING A POLE

To start with, we'll only use one pole on the ground. The longeur keeps the horse at the trot, as the rider goes to half-seat position, resting her hands on either side of the horse's neck and allowing her weight to sink deeply into her heels. The horse likely won't break stride; the rider will only feel the horse lifting his legs as he trots over the pole. Most importantly, the rider should practice staying in balance without the help of her hands. Her body should remain centered over the saddle. Once she's trotted over the pole a few times uneventfully in both directions, she can try the pole exercise in half seat with her arms stretched out to the side. And if all this is still going well, and the rider remains balanced over the pole in her half-seat position with arms outstretched, it's time to add a little bit of a leap.

CANTERING THE POLE

Ask the horse to canter immediately after trotting the pole. The rider should go into her half-seat position, cantering along for a full circuit. The horse should maintain the canter rhythm but find his own distance to the pole. The horse might stumble over the pole a time or two; he may leave the ground too far away and have to reach to clear the pole, or he may come right up to it before leaving the ground. He may even pick up the pace when he catches sight of the pole. Nevertheless, the rider stays in her half seat with her heels down and her hands planted in the horse's neck to stay with him.

An experienced horse will eventually find his stride and canter the pole just as if it was a small jump. The longeur needs to watch the rider's lower leg and upper body. It's a lot to take in at once. Both the rider's lower leg and her torso should stay steady and stable, with legs remaining underneath her. Watch, too, that the rider doesn't jump ahead of the horse in anticipation. You'll be able to tell because she will appear as if she's moved up the horse's neck. Her seat will no longer be over the center of the saddle. Some riders, especially those who ride with longer stirrups, have a tendency to wait too long before shifting their position slightly forward. In this case the back of the saddle can become a reminder to stay with the horse. The rider who is thus "left behind" will also feel her upper body snap backward on the landing side of the leap, and the cantle of the saddle may actually hit the rider in the seat of her pants.

Although this pole exercise is a lot of harmless fun for riders who are interested in learning to jump for a change of pace, it can also be an excellent position reminder for those who are serious about jumping; either those who need some position reinforcement, or want to improve. The experienced jumper rider can work on timing and position over the pole, while the longeur keeps a keen eye on the rider's lower leg position.

We've removed the side reins for jumping. Here the horse is unchallenged by the very small cross rail and simply trots over it as he would a cavalletti.

Jumping Blind

As the rider can canter more comfortably and competently over the pole, she should try it with her eyes closed, taking the half-seat position a few strides before the pole, closing her eyes, and riding over the pole as the longeur controls the horse at the canter.

Riders who feel some nervousness about jumping frequently throw their bodies up the neck of the horse in anticipation of the jump. They'll benefit from working with their eyes closed. Nervous riders jump ahead, fall off, become more nervous, and get ahead of the motion, in a self-perpetuating and dangerous cycle. The rider who is nervous about jumping should have a neck strap, such as a stirrup leather, to hold onto. Have her close her eyes and stay in half-seat position with her hands on the strap. She's not allowed to open her eyes again until she is three strides past the pole, and she must count out loud.

This exercise also illustrates how it feels to have the horse's body close the angle of the half seat, rather than having the rider fold too much at the hip. With the rider's hands on the strap or the sides of the horse's neck, she'll be able to feel the horse's neck coming up to her. From three strides out, the rider takes the half-seat position. She counts down, "Three, two, one, jump," with her eyes open. Then she can try it with her eyes closed. Over time the stride-counting exercise can start from halfway around the circle and then from three quarters. It's a fun way to play with rhythm and distance as the rider practices the two-point.

As the rider becomes more adept at the exercise, she can take control of the pacing by adding a little leg and increasing the length of the canter stride around the circle to see if she can successfully regulate her own distances to the jump. To increase the pace and meet the pole from a proper distance, the rider and horse need to be good at the half-halting and pace-setting exercises from earlier chapters.

Jumping with Wings

Balancing exercises in two-point position can be extremely useful for all riders, whether they have Grand Prix ambitions or just want to canter around a field and not worry about becoming unseated. A favorite exercise is to have the rider practice riding around with her "wings out"—I don't mean flapping elbows,

Practice the half seat without reins. When the rider is ready, work on balance over the jump by spreading the arms out like wings.

but rather arms out to the side, stretched to keep the rider's shoulders up and sternum lifted. This is the real test of rider balance.

The rider completes a whole circle with her arms out, calves long, and upper body stable, while the horse canters over the pole. It's an almost unbeatable way to make sure she can maintain her position balanced over the horse's center, even under adverse circumstances, so she won't fall backwards and inadvertently yank the bit on landing. That's vital to having a two-point position that's not dependent on reins for balance.

Besides being gentle on the horse's mouth, the rider with such balance can adjust her crest release accordingly. A crest release is the intermediate rider's position of the hands on the neck of the horse during the jump. It serves a couple of purposes: One is to assure the horse has room to move his neck out and forward over the jump. Another is to give the rider stability. In a long crest release, where the hands are halfway up the horse's neck, the rider doesn't have to worry about closing her hip angle in the half seat, because the placement of the hands will put her in the right position. The crest release changes according to the rider, the horse, the size of the jump, and the experience of the pair.

For now, though, the rider and longeur can add steps incrementally. Getting into position two strides out, the rider puts her arms out to the side over the pole jump, and then returns gently to a full-seat balance. A rider who is having trouble staying up should try the exercise again with one hand on the horse's neck and one arm out to the side. Then she can gradually loosen her grip with the one hand until she's feeling confident enough to try it with the hand resting in the air slightly above the neck, then stretching both arms out. Also note that if the rider is having trouble balancing she may be bracing against her toes. Work on having her sink the weight more deeply into her heels.

Hands on Head

Another good balancing exercise involves the rider putting her hands on her helmet and her elbows out to the side. Riders who depend on their hands for balance find this exercise, like the wings exercise, challenging because they'll be forced to use their lower legs to balance rather than their hands and arms.

Keeping the eyes up is extremely important in jumping. The rider can use her hands on her helmet as a point of focus. Even though she won't be able to see them, she pretends she's looking at the palms of her hands on her helmet as the horse leaps the pole. She can use a gentle lift on her helmet to bring her chin up. Riding over a pole in this position creates muscle memory for later, when the jumps are raised and it's crucial the rider stays focused on the steps ahead, rather than the jump underneath her.

In the second phase, combine three of the arm exercises: While approaching the jump from three strides out, the rider has her arms to the sides. Over the pole she puts her hands on her helmet. After the jump she crosses her arms across her chest.

TWO POLES

If all is well, the rider and longeur can graduate to two poles. Here the longeur and rider should understand a bit about related distances in jumping. Simply set up one pole directly across the circle from the other pole. Start out trotting the poles in half seat. The longeur needs to regulate the size of the circle so the horse trots and canters over the middle of both poles—otherwise the distances will be off. The rider helps the longeur control the horse by steering with her leg aids. She will use a little more inside leg to push the horse toward the center of the pole if he's on the inside edge as she's approaching. She'll use outside leg to bring the horse to center if he's drifting toward the outside of the pole. It may be necessary for the rider to pick up both reins to help center the horse on the approach to the pole.

The longeur asks the horse for canter, and the rider remains up in her half seat for the entire circle, opening up her hip angle a little in between each pole. If the horse is maintaining a steady tempo, the jumps will come at the right distances and the horse won't stumble over them. If the tempo is changing during the circle or the horse is falling in or out, the horse may take off too far ahead or too close (chipping in) to the pole. The rider and horse maintain a steady rhythm, and while riding through the center of each pole, they ready themselves for the next one. If necessary the rider can open her hip angle a bit to shorten the stride or add leg to lengthen it, depending on the kinds of distance she's getting to the pole. In either case, the longeur's job is to watch the rider's position, assuring she maintains her half seat and follows the horse's forward motion, even if they misjudge the takeoff point.

Raising the Bar

If all is going well, it's time to raise the bar, so to speak. Begin this exercise with only one small jump, using jumping blocks or very short standards that won't interfere with the longe line. I prefer the plastic jumping blocks, because you can raise and lower the height enough to make the horse actually lift off the ground, but don't run the risk of getting your longe line tangled up in the standard. Begin with a very small cross rail, only a foot off the ground. Having a "x" in the middle gives the rider, the horse, and the longeur a center point to focus on. Also, there's something psychologically comforting about the cross rail, especially for the timid or frightened rider. Perhaps it's that it looks lower in the middle or is more inviting to the horse.

The sequence for jumping practice on the longe line is simple: begin with a pole on the ground, make it cross rail, and then an eighteen-inch vertical. The first jumps should always begin at the trot. If the horse picks up the canter a stride or two out, that's fine. Just have the rider follow along with whatever the horse is doing. The rider remains stable in her half-seat position. Sometimes a little height can be a bit intimidating for the rider, so take it slow. As the rider becomes more confident, she asks the horse to canter the jump, in the same way she did with the pole on the ground. It works quite well for the rider to repeat the same arm exercises—out to the side, on top of the head, even clasped behind the back and hands on her waist—over the little jump. Later, you can have the rider practice the jump without stirrups. It requires some leg strength, so the rider should return to full seat gently after the jump to rest during the remainder of the circuit. She'll also find that she won't come quite so far above the saddle jumping without her stirrups, which might feel a little awkward. It's actually an excellent way to feel, as well as stay with, the horse's jumping motion.

The small vertical demands a little more effort from the horse. The rider is allowing the horse's movement to close her hip angle.

Add a second raised jump on the other side of the circle. All the rider needs is about eighteen inches of height to feel the horse sit, arc, and land. Clever horses may eventually learn the jump isn't high enough to warrant an actual liftoff and may just trot or canter over it without actually jumping. As the rider and horse master these exercises, the longeur can raise the fence to two feet (the maximum height of most standard jumping blocks).

Over time, add up to three more small jumps at the edge of the circle, so the obstacles are set up as a cross with the longeur in the middle. This is a quite a challenging exercise, but one that teaches the rider about pacing and using her eye to direct the horse to the next jump. The rider will have to think about turning the horse continually over each jump.

Besides being fun, learning to jump on the longe line reinforces how important it is to ride with seat and legs, rather than the hands. For those who'd like to begin to jump, it teaches them to stay out of the way of the horse's mouth. The position over the poles can become solid before the horse and rider venture off the longe line, where they'll have to navigate turns without the help of the longeur.

Conclusion

Now that you've tried all these exercises on the longe line, I hope you'll make a regular habit of practicing them. Longeing is a terrific way to gain confidence, build muscles, get a workout, and spend time with riding buddies. Although riding is a fundamentally solitary activity, it also can be a team sport where friends can help each other become better riders with just a longe line, a willing horse, and a good attitude. Although becoming an accomplished equestrian is a lifelong endeavor, as I've learned, adding variety in the form of a weekly longeing session helps both parties along the road to mastery. I wish I had started longeing earlier, rather than waiting until my riding habits had become nearly indelible. So by writing this book, I hope I've encouraged you to find a partner with whom to longe. It's good for everyone.

Acknowledgments

Although I spent many hours practicing these exercises alone (on my desk chair and my horse) and then writing them down, I think of this book as a collaborative effort, even if the collaborators didn't know it at the time. As such, I have many people to thank for their contributions. First, my teachers: Janet Shurink, Dolly Hannon, Lindy Weatherford, Whit Watkins, Joanne Hart, Katy Lindberg, and Nicole Thuengen-Polligkeit. Next are the horse friends and students who've been guinea pigs, sometimes unwittingly. Valda Terauds, for one, worked on the longe with me for two years while I recorded our lessons. Portions of those lessons appear here. Tere Carr, of Tick Nock Farm, who I mentioned earlier, provided the ideas for the sequences, while Olga Sacassa both photographed and modeled for the book. Other models include Tere, Penny Avery, Michelle Murphy, Janice Tiche, and Jere Beredino, and the horses, of course: Northern Lights, Baleno, and Volare. My editorial assistant, Celestia Loeffler, knows a lot more about horses now than she did a year ago. The horse friends from Table Mountain Ranch in Golden, Colorado; Course Brook Farm in Sherbourne, Massachusetts; and Old Town Farm in Albuquerque, New Mexico, provided me with much friendship and support over the years.

Resources

Ballou, Jec. *101 Dressage Exercises*. North Adams, MA: Storey Books, 2005.

Benedik, Linda. *Yoga for Equestrians*. North Pomfret, VT: Trafalgar Square Publishing, 2006.

German National Equestrian Federation. *Lungeing: The Official Instruction Handbook of the German National Equestrian Federation*. Boonsboro, MD: Half Halt Press, 2007.

Harris, Susan E. *The USPC Guide to Longeing and Ground Training*. New York: Howell Book House, 1997.

Hill, Cherry. *Longeing and Long Lining The English and Western Horse*. New York: Macmillan, 1999.

Inderwick, Sheila. *Lunging the Horse and Rider*. Devon, UK: David and Charles, 2003.

Klimke, Ingrid and Reiner. *Cavelletti: Schooling of Horse and Rider over Ground Poles*. Guilford, CT: The Lyons Press, 2000.

Savoie, Jane. *Crosstrain Your Horse: Simple Dressage for Every Horse, Every Sport*. North Pomfret, VT: Trafalgar Square Publishing, 1998.

———. *More Cross-Training: Build a Better Performance Horse with Dressage*. North Pomfret, VT: Trafalgar Square Publishing, 1998.

Swift, Sally. *Centered Riding*. North Pomfret, VT: Trafalgar Square Books,1985.

———. *Centered Riding 2*. North Pomfret, VT: Trafalgar Square Books, 2002.

Von Dietze, Susanne. *Balance in Movement: The Seat of the Rider*. North-Pomfret, VT: Trafalgar Square Publishing, 1999.

Index